DARK CONCEIT

Dark Conceit

THE MAKING OF ALLEGORY

EDWIN HONIG

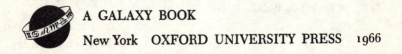
A GALAXY BOOK

New York OXFORD UNIVERSITY PRESS 1966

For Abraham Honig

and Jane Freundlich

Preface

THIS book explores the methods and ideas that go into the making of literary allegory. The first chapter estimates the biases that obscure the subject, then proposes a different view. The second chapter surveys the changing concept of allegory from a perspective that leads into our own times. In the third chapter the focus is on the typical constructs of allegorical narration, and in the fourth chapter, on allegory as a problem for its makers. The fifth chapter follows the development of three essential verbal modes in allegorical fiction. And, because the best allegory embodies an ideal which is integral to its methods, the final chapter discusses the role of such ideals in allegory and in related types of fiction.

No book of this sort can pretend to give the whole story about allegory. Too little is known, and almost nothing has been written about the subject which does not betray the parochialism of the specialist or the biases of nineteenth-century criticism. Although excellent books on symbolism are available, few—and those only fragmentarily—see the subject in terms of literary creation and literary criticism. The present study deals critically with allegory, and hence moves in an area where the scholarship has not yet been organized. The center of gravity is a group of Romantic and contemporary writers—among them Melville, Hawthorne, and Kafka—who continue the allegorical tradition in literature. Spenser and Bunyan are included because a useful description of allegory in our period cannot afford to omit them. They start the English Protestant evangelical tradition, with its popular kind of Biblical typology, which links them in many different and significant ways to Melville, Hawthorne, and Lawrence. Swift, though not in this tradition, belongs here too because, like Spenser's and Bunyan's, the core of his allegory is critical and self-embattled. His satire often finds a natural and nearly equal counterpart in Kafka's; together their works tell us almost all we can learn about the confluence of allegory and satire in fiction.

Early bearings on the subject were taken in an essay concerning the treatment of epic in Spenser and Joyce, and in another on the analogue of the Dionysus myth in Henry James' stories. A small part of that material appears here; the articles themselves are "Hobgoblin or Apollo," in *The Kenyon Review*, Autumn 1948, and "The 'Merciful Fraud' in Three Stories by James," in *The Tiger's Eye*, Autumn 1949. A version of Chapter Six appeared in *The New Mexico Quarterly*, Summer 1953, as "The *Ideal* in Symbolic Fictions." Of Chapter Four a substantial portion in earlier form was printed in *The Journal of Aesthetics and Art History*, December 1957, as "Re-creating Authority in Allegory." The last section of Chapter Two and the postword appeared in different form as "In Defense of Allegory," in *The Kenyon Review*, Winter 1958. I appreciate the courtesy of the editors of these publications in permitting me to use this material again.

I am grateful to the John Simon Guggenheim Memorial Foundation for the fellowship which gave full rein to my early curiosity about allegory. I am also grateful to the students of Comparative Literature 103 at Harvard University for the radiance of their responses, especially at those times when I had doubts that the subject even existed. Without such encouragement I should probably not have felt the challenge to start this book.

I must record my thanks to William Alfred, Milton Hindus, Kenneth Lash, Harry Levin, Milton Miller, Patrick F. Quinn, and Radcliffe Squires; I admired and tried to take into account their many fertile suggestions for various versions of the manuscript. I owe much to Richard Ellmann's sympathies and un-biased resistances, and to Northrop Frye, whose personal reas-surances and Promethean labors in all areas of literary criticism confirmed my sense of the shape which the book had to take.

The person I owe most to goes unnamed; my indebtedness is so evident to me on every page that mentioning her name here would be less than sufficient, and, the conventions of authorship being what they are, to say more would surely be mistaken for blind devotion.

EDWIN HONIG

Puerto de Alcudia, Spain
January, 1959

Contents

VI *The Ideal,* 147

In Sum, 179

If there be nothing new, but that which is
Hath been before, how are our brains beguil'd,
Which, labouring for invention, bear amiss
The second burden of a former child!
O! that record could with a backward look,
Even of five hundred courses of the sun,
Show me your image in some antique book,
Since mind at first in character was done!
That I might see what the old world could say
To this composed wonder of your frame;
Whe'r we are mended, or whe'r better they,
Or whether revolution be the same.
   O! sure I am, the wits of former days
   To subjects worse have given admiring praise.

SHAKESPEARE, *Sonnet LIX*

I

Foreground

Begin, ephebe, by perceiving the idea
Of this invention, this invented world,
The inconceivable idea of the sun.

You must become an ignorant man again
And see the sun again with an ignorant eye
And see it clearly in the idea of it.

Never suppose an inventing mind as source
Of this idea nor for that mind compose
A voluminous master folded in his fire.

How clean the sun when seen in its idea,
Washed in the remotest cleanliness of a heaven
That has expelled us and our images.

The death of one god is the death .of all.
Let purple Phoebus lie in umber harvest,
Let Phoebus slumber and die in autumn umber,

Phoebus is dead, ephebe. But Phoebus was
A name for something that never could be named.
There was a project for the sun and is.

There is a project for the sun. The sun
Must bear no name, gold flourisher, but be
In the difficulty of what it is to be.

WALLACE STEVENS, *Notes toward a Supreme Fiction*

THERE is a pervasive feeling against allegory, which, like most stubborn biases, springs from a mixture of distaste and half truths. The feeling is that allegory lends itself to polemical purposes and therefore turns inevitably into an exercise of subliterary fancies. Although the term allegory derives innocuously enough from the codifications of classical grammarians, its use as a concept develops diversely through the adaptations of philosophers, theologians, and literary men, impelled by conflicting interests and the exigencies of a particular occasion. Allegory comes to be thought a makeshift principle—at most, a very minor literary form—incidental to the issues which engendered it. Critics scorn it as a pedestrian notion somehow attached to a few masterworks by which it got in through the back door of literature.

If it were asked why allegory is so conscientiously mistrusted while speculations about symbolism abound as never before, one might say that in a scientific age allegory suggests something obvious and old-fashioned, like Sunday-school religion, but symbolism suggests something esoteric and up-to-date, like higher mathematics. It is a glib answer but not too far from the sources of the modern prejudice. Allegory is of course uncongenial to readers who find in it only an occasion for loquacious moralizing. But no one has yet shown that allegory is inherently of that crude type or why symbolism, for which critics always claim large potencies denied to allegory, is a superior literary practice. The Romantics were the first to exploit theoretical distinctions between allegory and symbolism as part of the larger campaign they fought to disentangle themselves from all rationalistic predeterminations. Encrusted on these distinctions are the accumulated biases of definition-making and the sanguine belief that allegory as a reputable literary form cannot have survived the industrial revolution.

Other reasons for the attitude against it grow out of the assumption that allegory is an artificial formula, the product of disjunction between the workings of reason and the workings of the imagination. Traditionally this view owes something to the classical rhetoricians, who saw allegory mainly as a device in persuasive argument. Even more is owed to the medieval analogical tradition, which regarded allegory as a trope containing a doctrinal truth. And so, while the other tropes—metaphor, irony, metonymy, synecdoche—even when quite strained, are customarily accepted as poetically gratifying, allegory, a more extensive figure that lends itself to narrative, comes to be known for its hortatory and prosaic qualities. Dante's prescription for allegory in the Can Grande letter reaches beyond these delimitations. He discusses allegory as a form of narrative fiction, saying that the style must be transumptive—that is, characterized by a poetic and rhetorical use of language—and that the method of narration must be digressive and episodic. This statement and the *Commedia* itself are precedents for considering allegory an organic literary type in which tropes function purposefully within the larger fictional scheme. In Dante's example and most later allegories, we recognize a distinct anagogical purpose, which the form and tropes fulfill.

In allegorical fiction certain recurrent devices serve to dilate or condense meanings exactly as tropes do in poetry. But so much depends on their circumspect employment that a lapse of skill can threaten the imaginative balance and turn the work into a sermon or a word game. For the critic such lapses only betray the inherent flaws in allegory. And this contention is presumably strengthened by his finding a more implicit use of correspondences in what he calls symbolic fiction.[1] So the question of technical skill, which should cover the writer's management of all fictional materials, is reduced to a question of his intention: the greater explicitness or transparency of intention showing allegory's inferiority to symbolism as literary procedure.

But nowadays symbolism is a more bedeviled, certainly a more diffuse, term than allegory. Semanticists, for example, continually warn us that the realm of symbolism includes nothing less than all verbal utterance. If one follows this view, in the way its proponents do who take literary symbolism to be the incessant use of figures of speech, then the meaning of a work becomes comprehensible only when the text has been broken down into a concordance of symbols. At best, this would be exchanging the work for a concordance. The term allegory fits the fictional procedure more accurately. From an allegorical view we can follow certain traditional storytelling devices which focus attention on the developing fictional scheme rather than the fortuitous arrestments of the language itself. There is little difference between the current semantic view which skims symbols from fiction and the nineteenth-century notion that allegory, a debased kind of symbolism, moves implacably along on two fixed lines of meaning and uses the narrative only as a convenient conductor for the moral lesson. The insistence on a disjunction between the "inside" and the "outside" succeeds only in isolating a rather barefaced kind of personification allegory. A good allegory, like a good poem, does not exhibit devices or hammer away at intentions. It beguiles the reader with a continuous interplay between subject and sense in the storytelling, and the narrative, the story itself, means everything.

Opinion about allegory in literary histories is fairly unanimous: most agree that it is dead but disagree about the date of its demise. Some say it withered away during the nineteenth century in Hawthorne's fictional hothouses and Tennyson's poetic isles and palaces. Others insist it died during the late sixteenth or early seventeenth century: already moribund in the morality plays, it shook spasmodically in *The Faerie Queene,* and gave up the ghost in Jonson's highly contrived masques. Another opinion has it that allegory was dying when Dante wrote his *Commedia,* and that it was precisely this poem which immolated both the literary form and the concept of allegory in one final flame. The validity of these opinions depends on each critic's assumption regarding the nature of allegory. It is no paradox to say that all are wrong and yet each tells us something important about allegory.

One thing they tell us, or at least generally imply, is that a distaste for the *idea* of allegory goes back a long way in the history of Western thought. This distaste is expressed in the *Republic* (which nevertheless contains the allegory of the cave) in Plato's remark about the long-standing quarrel between philosophy and poetry. It becomes obscured as the quarrel recurs and spreads, but the basic attitude persists. It is opposed to a way of thinking about the nature of reality as being something other than—that is, essentially against—what the senses or the reason affirms as evidence. But this prejudice is itself confounded by the fact that allegory has often been used and abused by the very philosophers, including Plato, who question its mystical, religious, or superstitious sanctions, and by the theologians who inveigh against the impieties of both philosophers and poets. Many Renaissance poets found in allegory the means of achieving structural design in epics; others impugned it as an esthetic heresy. Hawthorne and Melville sensed in it a viable fictional method instructive to their purposes. Coleridge, Poe, and James proscribed it as a device that destroys the integrity of a fiction. Critics who outlaw it today are themselves ardent letter hunters and sifters of intentions in Joyce and Faulkner, indicating that the same rattling of brains goes on that made the history of allegory so disturbing in the past.

There are clearly two central prejudices against allegory. One is a prejudice against the concept of allegory as a philosophical or rhetorical weapon, and the other a prejudice against allegory as a form of literature. In discussing the subject, most critics compound these prejudices, often without knowing that they are doing so. There are sufficient reasons why it is not always possible to distinguish the two. The employment of allegory by many literary and nonliterary writers has given it a well-marked functional character. At certain points in cultural development allegory is an indispensable instrument of thought and belief. Essentially part of the impulse Aristotle calls metaphysical ("All men by nature desire to know"), allegory reveals a fundamental way of thinking about man and the universe. Emerging from myth and ritual, the concept is first engaged in the earliest battle of the books fought over Hesiod and Homer. It constantly reappears thereafter on the borders between religion or philosophy and art, serving to frame significant questions about the nature of illusion and reality. Although often confounded with the theoretical occasions of its use, allegory is more than an accident in the history of ideas. It is a common, often the most dramatic, means of articulating and diffusing ideas.

This wide utility becomes a disadvantage when one tries to appraise allegory as a literary type. The difficulty applies to all literary types, but to allegory and other symbolic types especially. Except for a fragmentary poetics derived from Aristotle and classical rhetoric, there was no full-scale esthetic concerned specifically with literary works until the eighteenth century. This is why literary problems are treated many centuries after exemplary works have been frozen in classical postures, and long after vital imaginative issues have been overlaid by all the biases which prevented a critical formulation earlier. These biases coalesce in a single bias: the habit of basing generalizations about literature on claims of moral or social priority. In following a set of beliefs which conceptualize and evaluate problems of conduct and feeling, the bias takes literature to be a proving ground for particular causes that have been treated either soundly or unsoundly in a particular work. Artistic "givens" are thus confused with ethical systems, and the hypothetical structures of art with principles of philosophical demonstration.

The idea that a work of art is an independent organic structure was voiced as long ago as the Sophists and Aristotle. But since the idea was usually drawn from examples in nature and such imitative processes as carpentering and flute-playing, the question of how a literary art proceeds is never thoroughly confronted in criticism. Even in the Renaissance, when discussions of language and poetics preoccupied educated men, criticism was little more than a game of principles winnowed from Aristotle, the Roman rhetoricians, and the later Neoplatonists. The claim was repeatedly made that the methods of poetry are distinct from those of history and theology. And this claim gathered prestige when urged by poets as important as Dante and Spenser. Yet behind their statements lurks the sense of the poets' constraint, as though repeating the classical formula would help to allay suspicions of literary heresy.

The notion that literature is an offshoot of moral philosophy is never completely shaken off. Even in our own time, theories about the autonomy of art are still greeted as heterodox and as a means of making art seem more important than it is. Critics and artists have therefore been forced to extremes: from those Romantics who held that art is the transcendent expression of the artist's ego to recent estheticians who chillingly demonstrate that like mathematics, art, the objective creation of a master craftsman, owes nothing to any discursive form of thought and has a nondiscursive logic of its own. Then the moral or sociological critic intervenes to remind us of the "social import" of art, and we are given the preachment that art is essentially one of several cultural disciplines with special obligations to perform "for the common good." That artists follow compulsions of a mixed and often indefinable sort, and that a concern with problems of form rather than moral ideas leads them back to the works of their predecessors are matters that are ignored but directly influence the structural developments and ethical determinations in a literary work.[2]

What is allegory? In so complex a matter a definition or a series of definitions will not even hint at its manifold uses and adaptations. One must take a broader view of the subject than most critics do—broader, and at the same time more attentive to the formal properties of many different allegorical works. But before such an approach is laid out, we shall have to agree upon what is meant by the allegorical quality in a particular work. If we are lucky, the work of exemplification may succeed where definitions fail.

More fundamental than a definition or a philosophical bias are the usages of custom. For custom—here personified by the serious but nonspecialized reader—uses literary terms less self-consciously than the critic; and although, or perhaps because, it uses them indiscriminately, it is slow to drop terms which have been battered or buried in ideological controversies. Critics themselves, lacking a comprehensive methodology which can embrace the techniques of all literatures, often do no more than adopt the counters and makeshifts to which custom readily resorts.

Certain works customarily called "poetic" or "dramatic" are not written in poetry or drama at all. Used in this way, the terms indicate admiration, and have little to do with a literary genre. The practice is generally frequent enough to be thought innocuous. We continually use common words as epithets to register approval or disapproval. Semanticists call them "purr words," and they are the clichés of every language. But to use the generic adjectives more accurately than custom permits, one must have something better than axiomatic notions about the genres. Not that one would want to drop terms like "poetic" and "dramatic" for being inaccurate; what is wanted is a fuller idea of each genre which would also cover the variety and effects of innumerable examples. Thus one would tighten and clarify the meanings beyond the cliché, and perhaps regain some underlying sense in which custom is right—as it frequently is in a derivative aspect touching hidden origins.

Suppose, then, one asks whether a particular passage in literature is allegorical or not. It immediately appears that the quality cannot be so easily agreed upon as in referring to this

"poetic" or that "dramatic" element in a literary work. First, because poetry and drama are firmly fixed and readily identifiable
as literary forms; secondly, because the tone which greets the
poetic or dramatic quality is denied the allegorical. But suppose one represses an opinion regarding "allegorical" and asks
whether in *Coriolanus* Menenius' famous body-versus-belly
speech [3] is an allegory or in any sense allegorical. The speech,
of course, is adapted from a passage in Plutarch's Life of Coriolanus. Plutarch calls the passage a fable, and Shakespeare follows him by reminding an Elizabethan audience that the speech
rehearses an idea well known to them: "I shall tell you/A pretty
tale: it may be you have heard it;/But, since it serves my purpose, I will venture/To scale't a little more."

A fair answer to the question, "Is the speech allegorical?"
would depend, first, on what Menenius' tale, derived from the
analogy between the state and the human body, purports to be
in itself, without particular reference to the play; second, since
it is crucially employed in the opening scene to dispel a riot,
how it is to be understood in the immediate context; and, finally,
because one hears it echoed in Coriolanus' fate at the end of
the play when the conspirators are supported by the Volscian
mob in killing him, how the tale relates to the total dramatic action whose hero is Coriolanus.

In all three ways it fulfills certain functions of allegory, and
hence is allegorical. Simply by itself, the body-state analogy
voices a traditional belief reiterated by Classical, Medieval,
and Renaissance writers. In this way, the analogy is a persuasive
figure incorporating a doctrinal truth. It sets forth the ideal op-
eration of government according to the status of different
classes of men living in society. In its appeal to the venerated
ideal, which all men are presumed to share, the speech succeeds. (Of course, Menenius' identification of the leaders of the
state with the belly distorts the old analogy, and thereby abuses
the ideal.) Also, the speech is allegorical because, like allegory,
it functions as a trope on at least two levels of meaning. The an-
atomical analogy makes of a civil insurrection and a physiologi-

cal disorder one and the same thing. With regard to the immediate action, where the point is to forestall the Roman citizens' mutiny against the patricians, and against Coriolanus particularly, the speech-analogy works further like allegory by identifying the contingent roles of all characters so far introduced in one dramatic aspect of their relationship. By comic extension the chief rabble-rouser becomes "the great toe of this assembly." His dissident cohorts are implicitly shamed into regarding themselves as the other toes or as rebellious "members." Coriolanus, the successful general, and Menenius, the popular senator, are associated with the benevolent belly: "the storehouse of the body" that sends food "through the rivers of your blood." The members ungratefully return "but the bran" for the "flour" with which the good belly has dutifully fed them.

In a further range of implication, Menenius' analogy points toward the crucial defects in Coriolanus, and thus prefigures the fate of the hero who is temperamentally unfit for his appointed role in the social order. The body-state analogy depicts the prevailing attitude toward society which even the mob understands—or at least can be teased and stirred into abiding by. And so with regard to the whole play Menenius articulates the "law," the dispensation by which any man living in an orderly society must thrive or fall. In this most inclusive way the speech is allegorical because like allegory it defines the limits within which all human actions are made intelligible. Outside these limits are the "folly" of mutiny, understood by the mob, and the desperate "pride" of the outlaw, which Coriolanus enacts.

The speech then is allegorical in itself, in relation to the immediate action, and in relation to the whole play. It is allegorical, not because it is didactic, but because it performs several distinct and essential functions in the play. Some may call the speech itself an allegory, but here and in what follows the term applies to the full-length, inclusively figurative work and to the literary type which comprises such works. Menenius' speech shows how an allegorical trope extends itself and, further, how it serves as a guiding motif in a longer work. In examining how it is used we get an acute sense of the impulse to action it presents as well as the dramatic tension arising from the vital belief embodied in the analogy. Set forth in an early part of the play, this guiding motif prepares us for what is to come in the total resolution at the end. Shakespeare provides such motifs in the first acts of many plays: Ulysses' speech on "degree" (*Troilus and Cressida*); Edmund's soliloquy on "the foppery of the world," following Gloucester's portent of "the king that falls from bias of nature" (*King Lear*); Prospero's initial soliloquy spoken while Miranda lies in a trance (*The Tempest*), and so forth. Though none of these speeches is allegorical, like Menenius', they exert a similar pressure of figurative predetermination in the plays.

[*3*]

We find the allegorical quality in a twice-told tale written in rhetorical, or figurative, language and expressing a vital belief. In recognizing that when these components come together they form the allegorical quality, we are on the way to understanding allegory as literature. The twice-told aspect of the tale indicates that some venerated or proverbial antecedent (old) story has become a pattern for another (the new) story. Rhetorical language is the most appropriate one for telling the story because such a language produces self-reflective images—that is, its figurative character makes possible the retelling of the old story simultaneously with the telling of the new one. The belief expressed in the tale is the whole idea supporting the parabolic way of telling and the reason for the retelling; the belief binds the one with the other, as a resolution and its hypothesis are bound together. The relating of the new and the old in the reflective nature of both language and theme typifies allegorical narration. The tale, the rhetoric, and the belief work together in what might be called a metaphor of purpose. This is not another name for the moral lesson or for some momentary and narrow purpose. As we have seen, Menenius' speech-analogy relates directly to the main action of the play to which it is a thematic foreshadowing. It is also a set speech or virtuoso piece, having the same purpose as a good metaphor: to round itself out agilely in its own terms, and thereby improve the tale in the telling.

There is a pivotal relationship between the metaphor of purpose and the particular ways the writer uses an ideal and creates a new authority in the allegory. The implications of this relationship for the creative process in allegory are discussed at length in Chapters Four and Six. Here the relationship is described in a series of generalizations only to show the importance of this area in the preliminary approach to allegory which follows.

An allegory succeeds when the writer's re-creation of the antecedent story, subject, or reference is masterful enough to provide his work with a wholly new authority; such an achievement draws deeply on his ability to project an ideal by manifold analogies in the larger design of the whole work. The subject matter already stands, in whatever form, as true or factual by common acceptance. When the subject is taken over by the writer—particularly the allegorical writer, the author of a twice-told tale—it bears a certain general but muted authority, mythical, religious, historical, or philosophical, depending on the range of its acceptance. To come alive, the subject must be recreated, completely remade, by the writer. To remake the subject the author creates a new structure and, inevitably, a new meaning. To the extent that the subject is thus remade, it exists for the first time and has an authority independent of that of the antecedent subject.

The achievement of such authority comes about through the author's management of a dominant view—the ideal. The ideal is, variously or altogether, the theme of the work, the central concept adapted from a system of beliefs, or a subject matter which serves as a principal trope and which the whole work "proves" or fulfills. In effect the ideal is a pervasively animating force and, like the medieval anagoge, is the end toward which the whole work tends. Thematically and tropically, the ideal activates the purpose of the allegorical fiction. Although the ideal may be extricated from the work and evaluated, its existence as a recipe for action or a pious hope has little to do with the existential role it plays in the allegorical work. Why this should be so need not detain us here, except to note that *Don Quixote* is justly famous for the overwhelming way it answers the question.

A comprehensive view of allegory can be mapped out in terms of form, genre-type, and style. This threefold approach fixes the full range of the subject, from the individual example to all the possible examples taken together.

An allegory's form is its complete, over-all design shaped by a particular, often historically determined, use of tropes, and by the narrative medium that conveys them. Form is what marks the work's unique existence as a literary production. The form of Book One of *The Faerie Queene* differs from the form of Kafka's *Metamorphosis:* one is a narrative poem intricately combining classical and Christian symbologies in the framework of a national epic; the other is a prose fiction inverting the elements of a beast fable with a mock-naturalistic narrative and framing a satire-eulogy on the suicidal Judeo-Christian conscience. To see allegory formally is to see it in a particular example, writer and period, for the actual treatment it receives within a prevailing mode or medium. The form of an allegory must also be the form of the medium (prose or poetry, drama or novel) conveying it. But in whatever medium, it is a form that characterizes the allegory as a totally achieved literary creation.

An allegory's formal existence is part of a larger existence it shares, generically and typically, with other allegories. The allegorical genre refers to the many different works that engage an ideal encompassing the problematic nature of human existence. Both ideal and problem infuse all narrative elements, and most prominently, the manifold and self-expanding subject, analogically developed: e.g., Dante's "state of souls after death" or Melville's "overwhelming idea of the whale." Generically, allegory includes works of different periods and literary forms, all emphasizing the symbolic development of the subject. And so the *Roman de la Rose* goes with *Rappaccini's Daughter; The Pilgrim's Progress* with *The Castle; Gulliver's Travels* with *Moby Dick*. As a composite of many examples, allegory is a genre; as one of several related kinds of fiction using symbols —epic, satire, and pastoral—allegory is a symbolic type. (The same order of relationship applies to tragedy and comedy: each is a distinct literary *genre* as well as a *dramatic* type.) We recognize the symbolic nature of allegory in any example when a correspondence is struck between the characterization, imagery and narration, and the total design of the work, following antecedent examples of literary usage. When there are many examples we have a set of conventions. Allegory shapes one set; epic, satire, and pastoral shape others. Frequently overlapping one another, the conventions of the symbolic types differ mainly in attitudes toward, and in treatment of, cultural ideals. (This, again, is similarly true of tragedy and comedy with regard to attitudes and treatment of dramatic conventions.)

The distinctive style of allegory is an admixture of tonal elements, perhaps best illustrated by the medieval idea of a "middle" style, where "high" and "low" are combined for a unified effect. This style originates in the philosophical dialogue and Plato's fables; Ovid, Cicero, and Prudentius supply models for its later use in the Renaissance. Dante's letter to Can Grande describes its adaptation in the *Commedia*. The middle style, Dante explains, may be observed especially in the digressive and episodic movements of the narrative. "Digressive" relates to the dialectical form of inquiry involving at least two speakers; "episodic," derived from epic and drama, relates to the narrative procedure which sets forth and develops thematic exemplifications crucial to the symbolic unfolding of the story. In allegory's stylistic mixture of serious and comic (including the ironic) tones, one discerns the interplay of elements suggestive of satire, pastoral, the realistic or verisimilar (formerly the epic) sense, and the tragic sentiment. This is the style of Kafka's and Joyce's mature fiction, of *Don Quixote, The Faerie Queene* and *The Tempest,* and of the better allegories of Hawthorne, Faulkner, and Camus.

The threefold approach to the subject—formal, generic-typical, and stylistic—opens on the comprehensive possibilities of its methods and scope. This is not to indicate that everything is allegory or to press the case for it against symbolism, but to show how allegory, in transmuting powerful feelings and ideas in fiction, achieves homogeneity as a literary creation. Since its literary evolution is so heavily influenced by engulfing conceptual uses, the subject itself dictates that the way into it begin with an examination of such uses.

II

Conception

The first idea was not our own. Adam
In Eden was the father of Descartes
And Eve made air the mirror of herself,

Of her sons and of her daughters. They found themselves
In heaven as in a glass; a second earth;
And in the earth itself they found a green—

The inhabitants of a very varnished green.
But the first idea was not to shape the clouds
In imitation. The clouds preceded us.

There was a muddy centre before we breathed.
There was a myth before the myth began,
Venerable and articulate and complete.

From this the poem springs: that we live in a place
That is not our own and, much more, not ourselves
And hard it is in spite of blazoned days.

We are the mimics. Clouds are pedagogues.
The air is not a mirror but bare board,
Coulisse bright-dark, tragic chiaroscuro

And comic color of the rose, in which
Abysmal instruments make sounds like pips
Of the sweeping meanings that we add to them.

WALLACE STEVENS, *Notes toward a Supreme Fiction*

How does allegory get started? As a free literary invention that becomes allegorical only when the interpreter finds a separable body of meaning in the fiction? Or as the product of a conspiracy between writer and interpreter trying to make palatable a particular doctrine and thereby enforcing the reader's belief in it? And, after many ages of use and abuse, how does allegory manage to survive as a literary type into modern times?

Since the radical question of literary origins is unanswerable, one looks for evidence that may suggest an answer in a well-known historical instance: the early controversy over the Homeric poems. Here the conceptual nature of allegory shows itself typically in the work of interpreters trying to validate the contents of a traditional book without disturbing its form. Other questions about the general purposes of allegory may then be seen as related to such attempts to frame an ideal that defines an age's highest aspirations. And as we are interested in the implications of these questions for allegory in our own times, two further instances will be drawn from the interlocking developments of the theme of love and the esthetics of Romanticism.

1. The Traditional Book: Myth and Its Interpreters

In Book Ten of the *Republic* Plato refers to the old quarrel between philosophy and religion. Among other things, he undoubtedly had in mind the controversial eruption over the poems of Hesiod and Homer in the sixth century B.C. Xenophanes' complaint is familiar: "Homer and Hesiod have ascribed to the gods all deeds that are a shame and a disgrace among men: thieving, adultery, fraud." In answering the charge Theagenes and Anaxagoras asserted that the poetry is an allegory disguising certain moral and naturalistic truths in the persons and actions of the gods.

The Homeric poems and Hesiod's *Works and Days* had long been esteemed as sacred books; in them the Greeks found not only the lineaments of their history and customs, the tales of national heroes, but also their theogony, their bible. The poems identified a worship and a belief; as Herodotus put it, they "gave the Greek gods their names and portrayed their shapes." The importance of the allegorical interpretation was not simply that it sustained the integrity of the poems or its own pious defense of them against the combined scorn of Xenophanes, Heraclitus, and Plato. Had that been so, the interpretation and the poems themselves would have given way, as irrational anachronisms, to the new dispensations of Plato and Aristotle. What the allegorical interpretation upheld was the Homeric and Hesiodic view of man which sees all human weaknesses and heroism reflected in the gods. It made explicit what was implicit in the poems, the kinship existing between man and his divinities, by relating familiar archetypes to human aspirations which shape the godlike in man and the humane in gods. It did this by following a heightened ideal of individuality that had triumphed over a restricted, authoritarian worship in the domestic religion centered in the hearth and the ancestral tomb. In addition, the poems themselves passed into the Western tradition, so that new adaptations from them never cease to be made.

The situation is full of implications for allegory. One may infer, for example, that in the early phase of Greek philosophy the concept of allegory subjoins a convention of religious or mythical thought and establishes itself by defending the convention and prescribing certain precepts that underlie belief. Allegorical interpreters emphasize the "intentions" (in Homer and Hesiod, the ethical and naturalistic intentions) which they presume are inherent in a traditional text. Consequently the work of interpreters tends to preserve the text beyond the issues which call the moral nature of the book into doubt; in the process they also refashion the book's moral character to fit their own rationale.

The allegorical interpreter seems to take upon himself certain functions which have always been associated with the priest. And, whether he is officially invested with priestly prerogatives or not, a relationship between allegory and the interpreter's role is revealed which points back to an earlier religious practice when the prescribed values were so impacted in the worship that the two could not have been differentiated. The interpreter's role apparently expresses an earlier mythic fusion of belief with worship embracing fundamental ideals and customs upon which the structure of society depends.

In the domestic religion of Greece the father is the guardian of the family's social and religious obligations. The religion of ancestor worship, exclusive and secret in its rites, is concerned with the immovable hearth and the ancestral tomb. It is perpetuated through the apotheosis of the father on his death; in his worship the family is unified and the social law fulfilled. The hearth, where the sacred flame is kept burning, becomes the center of worship, sacrifice, vow-taking, and communion. Outside the house the fathers are buried and receive the family's perpetual libations. In this fixed orbit the religious and social order is maintained. The gods are functional but have no individual character; they are the dead fathers and the spirits having to do with the fire and its domestic uses. Through them the laws of inheritance, property, and marriage are determined.

Patriarchal and authoritarian, the domestic religion evolves into the religions of tribes and cities; its exclusive character is safeguarded by a hereditary caste of priests who are often heroes and kings. The hero and king display their authority on a wider scale: they preserve the religious rites and customs of large homogeneous groups and judge infractions of the laws. From the worship of the sacred fire in the family hearth to the worship of city gods, the priestly function remains pre-eminent:

to interpret signs, assemble artifacts and sacrifices, and maintain the law. Aeneas, Oedipus, and Orestes are heroes whose
different missions originate in special dispensations of a priestly
kind. They found cities, restore the favor of the gods, or start a
new worship. The later varieties of monotheistic religions are
built around the image of a sacrificed god or a man-who-be-
comes-a-god whose worship is sustained by the rites and prescriptions of a priestly caste.[1]

Hence the interpreter, as we may envisage him in the sixth
century B.C., is identified with an earlier privileged class of
guardians, primitive fathers, heroes, and gods. Like them he
seeks to preserve the images of authority and the transcendence
of cultural principles. Later such principles and authority are
linked to more complex cosmological issues: the workings of nature gods in the Olympian pantheon, and then the questions
which preoccupy the philosophers seeking more rational and
comprehensive ways of understanding the relation of men to
their social destiny.

In early philosophical systems ethical, psychological, and
scientific determinations are always contingent on matters of
social polity. When, as philosopher, the interpreter becomes a
more objective witness of nature and human conduct, it is clear
that he is thus putting into a new form the powers of the priest
who was himself an agent of the forces he shaped by rite and
worship. By bringing natural and transcendental forces together in a text, a ceremony, or a dance, the earlier interpreter-
priest confirmed an action and prescription which transfigured
belief in its mythical context into a sacred mystery.

This recalls certain features of allegorical interpretation
which persist to our own time. There is a resemblance between
the endowed quality of the mystery in myth and the allegorical
quality derived from a text. In each instance the quality has a
special appeal which, like color or size, distinguishes it. R. R.
Marett's description of myth as mana grown picturesque [2]
shows how this works. Mana, as the significant part of an object,
gives it extraordinary power. Like allegory in a sacred text it

evokes meanings and functions other than those immediately apparent on observation. These meanings remain inseparable from the object and from what the senses tell one it is. Like allegory mana means nothing if the spectator does not recognize its existence in the object. The priest endows the object with mana and the communicant apprehends its existence there. The object with mana, like the religious allegory, becomes an instrument of faith, something to worship, an artifact. If, as in Christianity, for example, a single god has created the text as well as the world, the text is the means of apprehending the presence of divinity in nature; there is "the good book" and there is "the book of nature" which it interprets. So, too, one might say of creations in art that they take on the quality of mana by lending themselves to many varieties of interpretation. There is also an obvious parallelism between object and mana, text and allegory, myth and mystery: in each case the original creation invites, is followed by, and frequently is wholly consumed by a variety of interpretative re-creations.

And so the questions, "Which comes first, the allegory or the allegorical interpretation?" and, "Which is which?" seem to some extent resolvable. For when we say that allegory is the created work having "purposes" which require explanation, we understand that both the allegory and its interpretation are fixed in one form by priestly practice. At an early stage allegory develops its appeal as a demonstrable mystery by existing intangibly in the worshiped object. To postulate the intangible as an energy working through the tangible helps to give the object life and meaning. The intangible quality is not separable from the object but suffuses it as motion in a stream or color in a leaf. So, too, the priestly prescription makes any differentiation between the myth and its ritual context virtually impossible.

Such practices identify the object by showing what quality or potentiality characterizes it, especially at a time when the power to name is equivalent to re-creating and controlling the object. Dominating the environment by precept and concept is typical not only of primitive thinking and the thinking of children but of all thinking and abstraction-making as well. Philosophical reasoning engages questions of opinion and judgment by formulating hypothetical principles. Poetic imagery hypothesizes on the basis of universal emotions and descriptive data. Mathematical demonstrations clarify and effect the transformation of reality through hypothesizing in numbers. All hypothesizing on first principles includes the problem of identification or name-giving.

To give anything a name, to call it this or that, is always in some degree to *evoke* it—to bring it into existence by voice, or through the mind's eye by memory or recall—from a context which we presume is actual or fixed in all men's minds by the customs of language. Identification is a form of action and figuration which makes the name as mental event synonymous with the thing named. It enables communion and communication between men, a sharing through language of what is held basic to their living together.

In this light it is worth noting that the word allegory (Gr. *allēgoria*, fr. *allos + agoria*, "other" + "speaking") and the word symbol (Gr. *symbolon*, fr. *syn + ballein*, "with" or "together" + "to throw") become related through shifting usage to the word myth (Gr. *mythos*, "word," "speech," "talk," "tale") and the word mystery (Gr. *mystērion*, fr. *mystēs*, "close-mouthed," fr. *myein*, "to be shut"). *Mythos* is originally the *word*, the first *tale*, which Greek thought subsequently distinguished from the synonyms *epos* and *logos*. *Mythos* thus entails the activity of *allēgoria*—"other-speaking" or "speaking otherwise than one seems to speak"—as well as *symbolon*, the "throwing together" of word and thing. And the activity indicated by *mythos*, *allēgoria*, and *symbolon* is synonymous with, rather than contrary to, the activity indicated by *mystērion*, the unspoken, "close-mouthed," as established by sacred use.[3]

Behind the name-giving process and the formation of hypotheses, and behind the tendency to equate the tangible with the intangible, myth with mystery, and so on, there is the basic interest in gaining a foothold in what is known, and to some extent protecting oneself from portents and fears of the unknown. Ideation and figuration bring about some sort of initial control and stabilization of reality. On the basis of the myth and the identification of objects there develops a greater sensitivity to natural phenomena and their interrelations. So, too, in the poetic or philosophical hypothesis there is an endeavor to push beyond the borders of what one appears to know and to enter the unknown. For the primitive and the child, the mysterious nature of the unknown, being vaster and more encompassing, lends itself to simple mythification.

The concept of allegory, which leads to the interpretations of an object or text on the basis of the meaning which lies potential in it, hovers on the indistinct border between primitive mythological figurations and the more sophisticated structures of philosophical thought. And so the allegorical interpretations of Homer that accompany the first philosophical attempts to construct a rational picture of the world open directly on the various premises of subsequent Greek thought. But also, in giving Homer's text an authority which identifies the typical actions and purposes of men in society, the interpretations fix the traditional character of the book both as history and as poetry.

The Homeric poems became a traditional book, growing rather than diminishing in prestige, in response to two rationalistic notions. Both notions were moralistic rather than philosophically disinterested. The first advanced the tendency to consider the poems a document celebrating cultural ideals and national heroes of divine descent, with the implication that the poems were historically authentic. Like the Hebrew prophets, or like King Arthur's knights later, the persons and exploits of these heroes appealed to national pride. Following genealogical lore, the Greeks thought of themselves as descendants of the Homeric heroes. Families and tribes worshiped Achilles and Ulysses, whose names they took as patronymics. The second notion, typical of the allegorical interpreters, took the poems as a fiction and moralized the gods by giving them distinct physical and ethical functions. The gods were conveniently renamed for parts of the human anatomy and their battles made to dramatize physiological malfunctions. Their shifting alliances became an ingenious contest in the arena of good and evil. This notion is cautiously upheld as late as Longinus, who in discussing Homer's Battle of the Gods, finds it necessary to declare: "But although these things are awe-inspiring yet from another point of view, if they be not taken allegorically, they are altogether impious, and violate our sense of what is fitting." (The impiety makes "gods of the men" and "men of the gods.") Both historical and allegorical notions are united by Euhemerus in the theory that since the gods are deified men, the myths may be interpreted as traditional reports of historical persons and occurrences.

Whether taken devoutly or as an exercise in exegesis, the practice of systematizing myths seems essential to establishing their character in the traditional book. What is true of the Homeric poems may also be said of every great work of similar scope: the Bible, the *Aeneid,* the *Commedia.* They become traditional by attracting widely predicated systems of interpretation and belief. The commentary interprets the book's meaning, and is itself thereby assimilated into a tradition of beliefs which the book has solidified.[4] Thus, even if only through its dramatic interest, the book could impress upon men not simply why they act as they do but also how they might or should act.

Gilbert Murray has applied the methods of philological research to the problem of deducing the evolution of the early traditional book. He traces the pattern of its use and growth as a cumulative process of agelong emendation, expurgation, and accretion. The traditional book is an organic structure like a tree, which the historical scholar must read much as a plant physiologist reads tree rings. In uncovering what is still legible on successive layers, he learns something about the ways its nameless authors have shaped the book. All changes apparently correspond to an accepted and revered story. "If you take up the Iliad as a record of history," Murray remarks,

you will soon put it down, exclaiming, "Why, this is fiction!" But if you read it as fiction, you will at every page be pulled up by the feeling that it is not free fiction. The poet does not invent whatever he likes. . . . It was not the business of the bard to invent. It was his business to know, by information from the Muses or elsewhere, the history of the past, and to tell it to his new audience accurately, word for word, as the Muses had told it to him.[5]

This is what makes the book traditional—its many authors successively building upon the historical belief in eponymous heroes. Thus if "the whole basis," as Murray says, "is not fiction, but traditional history," one may assume that the poet's function in illuminating and transfiguring the history into poetry is more authoritative and independent than that of any commentator. By following the muses, by imagining well without trying to justify, by driving inward toward the mythically endowed core, the poet sustains the story's inviolability within the poem. The commentator moves outward from the poem to correlative ideas bred by all the controversies regarding its purpose. And so the commentator domesticates what he finds or constructs upon something in the work which lends itself to elaboration.

In this way the traditional book is also comparable with any work of single authorship around which a canon of interpretation has accumulated. Interpreters accomplish their revaluations from outside rather than from within the book. A particular interpretation in one age will seem more important, more necessary in a cause seeking cultural ascendancy, than the work itself,[6] whose accumulated meanings are then restructured to serve that cause. And in this respect Murray's view of the old epics as expanded lays reminds one of the notion of allegory as expanded metaphor and as an interpretation of mystery expanded outward toward particular dogmas, when the mystery or allegory takes on the semblance of a religious artifact.[7]

2. *The World as Text: Shifting Current of the Ideal*

Homer enters literary tradition on being disengaged from a restrictive theogony by the philosophers. Yet the heroic values which endure in the Homeric poems are constantly recalled in the ethics of Greek philosophers. Homer's characters and their problems grow into literary archetypes through the adaptations of Greek dramatists, the revitalized mythologies of the Roman poets, and the renewed sanction Virgil gives the epical hero proceeding on a national-religious quest. What have these things to do with allegory and the interpretation of allegory?

The concept of allegory assumes a subject sacred to belief or revered in the imagination. The world—any part of it—may provide the text: a running stream, a solar eclipse, the orderly flight of birds. A body of doctrine, whether mythical, religious or philosophical, first identifies the subject in order to place or elevate it in a specific context of ideas. The doctrine ascribes to it a function in time, which relates past, present, and future in a predictable way. When two such subjects are identified, the implication of some relationship between them is indicated. The categorizing of subjects on an evaluative scale of definition is a recourse of the mind seeking to fix relationships. As the number of subjects increases it becomes necessary that the identity and function of individual subjects coincide at every possible point with the identity and function of the whole, especially where the whole is thought to include all its parts and to represent in itself a key concept.

In Plato and Aristotle the instruments of philosophic constructions expressed by triads and tetrads, together with the key concept of Idea or Form, impose themselves on the subject of inquiry so that the whole of nature and the ethical life seem to be pressed into shape by the doctrinal instruments. Without going into the related problems of logic and epistemology, one may regard the matters of name-giving and function-calling as stemming from a need of the imagination—the powers of dis-

cernment and intuition—to dominate what it cannot avoid en-
countering, with a unifying ideal. The nature of this ideal becomes the constant aim of reference to which all portions of the
text or of the whole subject must be related. The doctrinal ideal
conditions the way things are categorized and lends significance to the name-giving and function-calling processes. The
more compelling and flexible the ideal, the more far-reaching
the effects of the system will appear to be.

When these observations are applied to literary texts the same
habits of designating identity and function appear in the procedures of the author and his reader. A literary text which has
been assimilated in a cultural tradition requires a restructuring
from every reader. This occurs when the reader gradually reflects in his own imagination the creative process embodied in
the text. This restructuring of the text by each reader renews
the inner "consciousness" of the artistic work. Such re-creative
reading occurs, in different degrees, with each new reader of
any work whatever. The instances where this process is im-
peded are few, perhaps significantly so, as it is, say, with regard
to the Bible, where the text cannot easily be disengaged from
the religious dispensations and cultural habits which have suf-
fused it. One reads the Bible with the whole history of Christianity implicit in every verse and chapter; and since the experiences and commentaries of a whole civilization have become
layered upon the text, the Bible can seldom be freshly encountered by the individual reader.

A free development of rational and imaginative thought
is necessary for the continual growth and the analytic understanding of a literary form. Creative thought does not begin
without some subject, some sense of an already existing order—
in nature or in a text—which the mind designates by identity
and function. Speculation deliberately seeks to free the text of
its former commitments in order to make it personal and contemporary at the same time. Yet this never happens quite so
simply or completely since something of the old way of perceiving is inevitably accommodated to the new notion that tries

to replace it. Thus when history and philosophy encroach on myth or when the Homeric gods are superseded by the ethics of Plato and Aristotle, there follows a significant reformulation of the cosmos. The reformulation is inseparable from a new ideal which looks at the world quite differently. Then when this ideal is in turn challenged, and the formulation is again revised by the Christian cosmogony, the sense of the cosmos shifts anew. The process does not go on ad infinitum, however. As Greek thought merges with the strong current of Eastern dualism in Pythagoreanism and Platonism, it gradually becomes fixed in Western culture. Subsequently classical systems and doctrines are discarded, buried, or absorbed by the Church fathers, and then are pieced together and refashioned by Renaissance learning on their later rediscovery.

Growing along with Greek thought, the concept of allegory shares the fortunes of that thought. Engaged and anatomized by interpretation whenever the dominant ideal has been fixed by dogmatic belief, allegory is re-adapted by subsequent interpretation when the ideal changes. The literary form called allegory follows through the ages the imperatives of conflicting ideals rooted in the nature of thought and belief. When the allegorical form is scrutinized, one finds the evidence of its adaptations of appropriate, prior structural modes and symbolizations: elemental symbols, tables of basic contrarieties, concepts of dualism, triadic and tetradic categories, and all the philosophical metaphors used to demonstrate identification, motion, unity, and immutability. Myth and philosophy give allegory its themes and method; epic and drama prefigure its form; a traditional poetics defines its purpose; and religious doctrines ritualize it in heuristic formulas.

In Christian analogy allegory is given its most elaborate formulation. Answering the problem of justifying the Bible as both history and the Word of God, this formulation stabilizes and eventually rigidifies the concept of allegory for more than a thousand years. We are not here concerned with tracing these developments. In the 1,500 years between Alexander and Aquinas, allegory was used mainly to meet the demands of theological controversy. And apparently when allegory is employed for polemical purposes significant literary allegories are not produced. It is mainly through the *Commedia* that allegory finds its way into the mainstream of literature. Dante's achievement was to revitalize the basis of Christian analogy and to restore the ideal of the timeless present, so devoutly projected by medieval philosophers and theologians, as an immemorial reality in art.[8] Through further amplifications of its ideals,[9] the concept of allegory infiltrated many literary forms. Two vivid amplifications are the exploitation of the theme of love, following the conventions of the medieval courtly poets, and the typical Romantic view of art and the hero, detailed by Kant and Coleridge. Though occurring centuries apart from one another, the earlier development closely involves, and possibly even culminates in, the later development. Together they bring us within range of the contemporary period, where the use of symbolic techniques becomes the dominant literary preoccupation.

3. *The Ideal of Love: Natural Woman Redeemed*

It is often noted that among the early matriarchal religions of the Mediterranean and the Orient the chief deities were goddesses of fertility, love, mercy, and beauty. In striking contrast, the whole Western tradition kept woman rigorously subservient in its religious dispensations.[10] In Genesis she brings sin into the world (Eve), and at the moment of salvation yearns for the infamous old life (Lot's wife). She is known for her wiles, whether selfish or altruistic (Rebecca and Esther), and for her fatal seductiveness (Delilah, Judith, Susanna). At best she belatedly engenders a nation (Sarah) or becomes a paragon of domestic piety (Ruth). The traditional morning prayer of the orthodox Jew rings with a sentence thanking the

Almighty for not having created him a woman. Still unredeemed when she appears in the Gospels, she must deny her nature in order to conceive the Messiah. And when we meet her in Revelation, she is the ignominiously triumphant Whore of Babylon as well as the mother of the Messiah. Even as late as the fourth century, the Virgin is assailed for vainglory by St. Chrysostom.

The Greeks who praised boys thought her shrewish if not despicable. For them love is a soul seeking a body or a courteous exchange between intellectual equals. Catullus, Propertius, Apuleius and Ovid often depict sexual love as a public exhibition, a form of female madness, or a coarse joke. Among heroic Romans and medieval epic heroes, love is frequently a profession of mutual joy from the lips of dying enemy warriors. Directly responsible as she seemed for the Fall of man, the erotic nature of woman was considered her prime defect and attraction; hence she was barely tolerable to the early Christians, even under seal of the marriage contract.

At the turn of the eleventh century a rather different and more complex attitude emerged. Indirectly inspired by the cult of the Blessed Virgin, poets celebrated a new ideal of sexual love. The ideal expresses a departure from the earlier, dehumanized view of woman. The Virgin Mary had intermittently served as a merciful intercessor between man and the authoritarian Trinity. In softening the severity of his fate she was gradually turned into an object of religious worship. In this role she seemed partly to condone Eve's sin. But the worship was limited to the Virgin alone; it did not shake off the old prejudice concerning the base nature of woman generally. In exalting the extra-marital liaison between a lady and her vassal knight, poets of the courtly ideal were solemnizing not the erotic fulfillment of a beautiful relationship but the customs of fealty and courtesy which preserved the disparity between the lovers' stations. This is especially evident in the romances when the beloved is socially superior to her lover. The idealization sublimated the fiat of obedience linking servant to mistress and proved through the lover's heroic action. (Possibly it is this relationship, with all its social implications, that made the ideal so easy to satirize later, as, for example, in the reversal of social stations when Don Quixote dedicates his quest to the kitchen wench Dulcinea.)

In the Arthurian stories and the Rose legends the knight's goal is half mystical and symbolic, half sexual and wondrous. The beloved usually inspires the main action by instigating the mission and the knight's adventurous appetite with the promise of herself as reward. Consequently when the theme of romantic love came to be exploited in European literature, it offered an idealized view of woman as forbidding in her eminence as she had been before in her abasement. The sense one gets of this ideal is affected by the ambiguous way she is made to fit her uneasy role. Pervasive and inaccessible at the same time, initiating but having almost no part in the quest itself, she is portrayed as sexually desirable, yet only as a porcelain beauty is, being more adored than gratifying. Exhibiting traits compounded of the Sibyl, the fruitful Eleusinian Demeter, and the more ruminative Lady Philosophy of Boethius, she lurks on the border between man's highest abstractions and his resolute desire for some heroic realization. The ideal does not sustain her comfortably except in the guise of a personified virtue in metaphysical debates; or, somewhat later, in the image of male passion foredoomed: a kind of Lady Death, her most glorious avatar, as she often appears in early Renaissance ballads and moralities.

The more sublimated the attitude toward her, the more dreamlike and attenuated is the atmosphere surrounding her, as in the first portion of the *Roman de la Rose*. When she is reduced to mere flesh and blood, the antagonism is reasserted and she is again anathematized, as in the second part of the *Roman*. The celebrated real-life tragedies of Paolo and Francesca, Abelard and Eloise, reveal the underlying fatalism as surely as the Tristan and the Don Juan legends do. Where the romantic love theme is made synonymous with the ideally possible, it provides a frame in which to cast a sort of sexual ethics. When love becomes visionary, through personal revelation and ascetic discipline, it shows the engrossed soul how to transcend the body and merge with God the Son. In either case the theme leads to clinical extravagances when the passion is broken down and reasoned out of its need for the love object.[11] The overidealized woman invariably evokes a religious sense of awe to which she is sacrificed as the fatal object. Being love's martyr and scapegoat, she is ultimately depersonalized; only the ideal espouses her. Excessive and ambiguous though it was, this view of woman held more promise than the more rigid, older attitude: possibly only in this way could she begin to be understood as a real human being.

The constrained view of woman quickened the impulse toward poetic and allegorical expression. It reawakened the *materia* of the older religions, which had treated woman as a creative force, and sanctified her according to the *misteria* of another kind of worship. Muse, mother, lover, and judicial principle, she was reconceived in each of these aspects of her older religious functions. As the incarnation of love she was subjected to the same exhaustive psychological and symbolic treatment that Augustine had devoted to questions of sin and salvation. Symbolic of love and grace, Dante's Beatrice is an earthly woman, a muse, and a worshiped goddess merged with the image of divine love. Thematically secured in this way, her role could then be particularized in later allegories where, if she was not always personally redeemed, she became increasingly significant in the hero's quest for redemption. Spenser, Hawthorne, James, and Lawrence are among the later allegorical writers who thus enlarge her role symbolically. And each in his own time seems to create a new sense of wonder out of a stubborn and apparently buried mystery.

The marvelous as such is impossible to define because it represents different things to different witnesses. But its effects are felt immediately by everyone. Since these effects are usually engaged by profound cultural biases for which we have no precise name, we recognize the marvelous most strikingly in archetypal myths. We respond to it, for example, when Prometheus is liberated from the rock and escapes the eternal punishment of Zeus, his persecutor. We find it symbolically enacted by Orestes in his flight from the Fates after murdering his mother. It moves us suddenly through the divine retribution Oedipus suffers by his own hand long after his forgotten patricide and life of incest. And we are swiftly struck by it in the scene of Christ's passion on the Cross, when He symbolically rises as from conflicting earthly and heavenly aspirations—the condition of every man pinned to the vertical and horizontal sticks of his being.

Archetypal situations of this sort apparently involve the dynamic interplay of two broad, antagonistic principles. One might say the conflict between these principles is nearly pervasive enough to affect every emotion and every move a person makes or thinks of making. Together these principles engender the dichotomies of art evolving out of authoritarian religion, and relate to the biases of artistic expression we call classical or romantic, rational or enthusiastic. One principle is the dominance of woman and the natural virtues imputed to her, which are culturally shaped into the matriarchal ideals of love, equality, peace, mercy, fecundity, the reassuring periodicity of nature, human freedom, brotherhood, and the world as an earthly paradise. In opposition is the powerful and now apparently victorious principle of male authority, which encompasses all the virtues of civilized life: law, conscience, justice, military heroism; the concepts of hierarchy, primogeniture, and individualism; and the material conquest over nature.

In his famous anthropological critique of "motherright," *Das Mutterrecht* (1861), J. J. Bachofen developed the sociological and ethical implications of these opposing principles. Bachofen's main interest was to apply them to the dynamics of Greco-Roman society: its laws and history, its familial and religious customs. Yet there are other implications of the "motherright" theory which reach into the ethical and esthetic realms of the world's greatest drama.

In this light, for instance, an important issue of the *Oedipus* plays is the contention between father and son overtly signalized by the problem of incest. Similarly the *Oresteia* portrays symbolically the last battle between the maternal and paternal deities for cultural ascendancy. After Orestes has killed Clytemnestra, who has murdered Agamemnon, the Fates, representing the matriarchal principle, pursue Orestes and call for his punishment. But the ascendant deities, Apollo and Athene, favor Orestes, so that the patriarchal principle, justifying the son's avenging of his father, finally triumphs.[12]

The contention between male and female principles also turns up in Elizabethan drama. In many of Shakespeare's plays one finds the same archetypal conflict at work in different ways. Perhaps in both the Elizabethan and Periclean periods the tragic sense of life is reflected in the breakdown of cultural taboos and hierarchic belief. The threat and the titillation which a playgoing audience feels on witnessing the result of such a breakdown challenge the deepest allegiances and defections. In restoring the communal sympathies of the audience, a purgation through pity and awe is precisely the safeguard society needs against attack upon it implied in the action of tragedy. Possibly only at the risk of imagined dissolution through the play's enactment of the most unspeakable catastrophes can actual or potential assaults against constituted authority be momentarily allayed. The archetypal myth—where the conflict between primordial forces is most intense, as between matriarchal and patriarchal values—supplies the great ages of tragic drama with the most effective subjects.

At several points in *The Tempest* one senses that the matriarchal virtues are at stake and that they eventually triumph. Repentance and mercy finally overcome treason and fratricide through Prospero's magic art. At the end a masque based on the Ceres-Proserpine myth celebrates the marriage of Miranda and Ferdinand; and the last scene significantly provides for a reconciliation between brothers. In *King Lear* the tragedy seems to involve an unprecedented defaulting of the patriarchal will and, in effect, a perversion of the matriarchal virtues, which it pretends to foster. Subsequently it is shown that the daughters Goneril and Regan are twisted and not "true" women, who turn Lear's freely yielded patriarchy into a tyrannous anarchy. By reversing their natures they become, as it were, vengeful sons. Cordelia, who is true and will not be twisted, is sacrificed by them to this perversion of patriarchal authority. There is a similar turnabout in *Macbeth*. In complying with a distorted ideal of woman (incited first by the three Weird Sisters—reminiscent of the Old Fates—and then urged on by Lady Macbeth), Macbeth converts the normal patriarchal order into the bloody chaos of an abnormal male-aspiring matriarchy. Something of the same reversal takes place in *Coriolanus*. The son's fitful and lopsided courage seems directly attributable to the education he has received from his mother, Volumnia, who is unnaturally obsessed with war and power. As it happens, the only human being Coriolanus can embrace passionately is the enemy warrior, Aufidius, who finally engineers his death.

In these examples the bias favoring the patriarchal principle is continually at odds with a matriarchal insurgence. Rooted in such situations is the Renaissance concept of social order, which assumes the monarch's absolute authority, tempered by humanistic and Christian virtues, and possibly also, in Shakespeare, by the aura of a female monarch. In *The Tempest* the Arcadian image projected on a remote enchanted island appears to favor the normal matriarchal virtues. The emphasis is modulated by the governing art of Prospero, whose magic benevolently follows a primitive Christian creed. At the end when Prospero breaks his staff and Arcadia dissolves, there is a plea in Prospero's request for their prayers that the dramatized Christian virtues be taken to heart by the audience. The archetype—in this instance, a primitive paradisal situation where the forces of evil are under control—is recast to fit the contemporary belief in a benevolent despotism founded on Christian virtues. In effect, the conflict between authoritarian principles and those of innocent love, mercy and repentance, is assuaged by a compromise which allows both sides a degree of victory.

The primordial forces made evident in the matriarchal principle are seldom permitted to emerge from the unconscious except when sublimated in some religious or artistic ideal. When art re-embodies them the principle is brought back to the consciousness as a blooded dream of possibility, a realizable ideal. Much of this sense pervades Goethe's *Faust,* and culminates in the celebrated final lines, *"Das Ewigweibliche/ zieht uns hinan."* The same ideal appears in the utopias of poets and philosophers, in the cult of the Virgin, and in humanistic and scientific pursuits, where the matriarchal virtues affirm and enrich the concept of man's dignity. When a great art re-creates the marvelous in these terms it comes not simply in reaction to the tremendous constructions of priestly authority or the systematic rationalism of surly idealists. On the contrary: the marvelous, especially when it grows out of a new ideal like romantic love, owes as much to a well-wrought theology with its psychology of sin and moral exclusivism as it does to rival heresies, dormant myths, and the need for a new spiritual affirmation. It owes at least as much to all these things as to the inexplicable appearance of several individual geniuses, a new way of using language, and a new sense of craft.

The intellectual vitality of the Renaissance subsists in its conversion of the classical, and its secularization of the Christian, ideals. The rediscovery of the past, the preoccupation with the virtues of "the whole man," and the exploitation of the vernacular encouraged the growth of realism and the proliferation of new literary forms. Art in pursuit of the sensory particular cast off the supererogatory constraints of medieval allegory. Except in Spenser, allegory did not seem to suit a narrative procedure which instilled realistic portraiture and enthusiastic heroism with modified notions of classical decorum. The caricatures of satire and the fascination for political Machiavellism tended to subvert the allegorical ideal. The appeal of an empirical attitude lay in the range of particularities it offered beyond the classical and Christian views. In anathematizing the universal it also cast off the system of signs and figures which had been the theological bulwark of medieval dogma. But later, when ultrarational and classicistic ideas became a literary addiction, essays in prose and verse affected the sheerest kind of personification allegory to dress out critical, political, and religious squabbles. It was away from this literary dead end and toward the new possibilities of an individualistic ethic, inherited from Renaissance secularism, that allegory turned for revitalization during the Romantic revival.

4. *Romanticism: The Autonomy of Art and the Hero*

In proclaiming the priority of the individual, the typical English Romantics saw in Christian analogy mainly the blandishments of a discredited priestcraft. Hunting for the true individual rather than the true faith, they celebrated the vitalism of existence and an heroic self-determination. The hero's quest no longer reflects the ethical norms of Aristotle or the metaphysics of Aquinas; it starts instead from a subjective notion of cultural rejection and moves toward the impasse of overreaching conscience.

This centering of doubt and ethical ambivalence made for little stability in philosophical terms. The typical classical and Christian hero functioned as a culture-bearer—a figure whose aims, ratified in a successful mission, were immediately apparent to the society whose talisman he carried. But the Romantics, disdaining mere success stories and pat views of salvation, revered the outcast, despot, madman, dandy, and intellectual superman. From types based on Prometheus, Orestes, Faust,

Hamlet, Don Quixote, and Don Juan, they created the heroic avatars of Napoleon, Byron, Peer Gynt, Wilhelm Meister, Sade, Captain Ahab, and Rimbaud. In retelling myths and legends, they dwelt upon uncommon traits, priding themselves on a catholicity of choice which could find heroic prototypes in every age without engaging their beliefs in the values of any one. Part of their hero's uncommonness was that, in belonging to all times and places, he, like the Romantics themselves, professed allegiance to none. He was the real cosmopolitan among the patriotic beggars and respectable middle class whose laws he overthrew, whose foibles and shams he exposed.

For the social hierarchy under God, the Romantics substituted an esthetic hierarchy based on the prerogatives of the man of feeling, the immoralist, the artist, the confidence trickster. The Romantics could easily dismiss the Lord of Creation for a God of Love, Sympathetic Nature, or the Demon of the Absolute. Instead of Bunyan's plodding Christian earning his heavenly reward by imitating the life of Christ, they invoked a monstrous egoist who lavishly loved woman, knowledge, power, or freedom more than the world, and who, when frustrated, sought to impoverish it by his suicide. Or, what came to the same thing, a rebellious strong-man prophet who remade the world in his own image and then brought the whole fabrication down with him in a last delirium of destruction. It did not matter in which class the hero had been born; it only mattered that in order to act he must be conscious of having been declassed by temperament.

Rejecting the eschatological symbols of Christian allegory, the Romantics found impassioned identity in free association, spiritualism, psychological empathy, folk superstitions, transcendental communication with the demiurge, the correspondences of nature, and the systematic derangement of the senses. Instead of the petrified personification symbol of debased allegory, they insisted on the Janus-faced metaphor, the ironic ambiguity, the self-contradictory hypothesis. Setting aside prescribed systems of axiomatic interpretation, they expounded the psychological or mythological brief which interpreted artistic creation as an original and self-inclusive act. And in opposition to the traditional view of the interconnectedness of form and matter, their theory and practice gave weight to the part over the whole, the emphatic digression as against the linear development of narrative and plot, and the significant inconclusiveness as against the well-prepared denouement.

The Romantic esthetic had arisen in different ways from Kant's critiques of reason and judgment. Kant's principal formulations deal with questions of subject-object relationships relative to a priori or a posteriori modes of reasoning, and to the prime forms of thought (categories) that mold all judgments. In moral and esthetic terms, however, it turns out that after dismantling the transcendental character of the unknowable in dogmatic philosophy, Kant replaces it with the self-determined character of man, who, by the power of his will and the subjective nature of the Ego, creates the beautiful and the sublime. And man gives himself the moral law, the categorical imperative: "Act so that the maxim of thy will can at the same time be accepted as the principle of a universal legislation." As the only discerning subject of experience, in whom the subject-object relationship imperceptibly merges, man raises the particular to the universal. And through the experience of art—a higher form of cognition and sensuous experience—man grows independent of nature.

Kant locates the ideas of the beautiful and the sublime in esthetic, and not in logical, judgment. They are effects of the imagination, which has no teleological purpose. In art they excite and satisfy by stimulating the free play of all perceptive capacities, and so come to represent an ideal esthetic norm which can be subjectively understood by all men. Through feelings of pleasure we gain access to the criteria of taste, which are functions of the understanding and reason. The beautiful pleases as a symbol of the morally good (the categorical imperative) and thereby incites the taste to judge ethical ideas in the sensible form of art.

The work of art has a purposefulness-without-purpose: in "function it is more like a tree or a flower than like a chair or a table." It is not separable, as it was for Plato or Aristotle, from the spontaneous (natural and necessary) character of man himself, who is both a thing-in-itself and a maker of art. Art for Kant is a representative expression of human freedom, submitting to no arbitrary restraints but evolving out of its own rules.

The principle that the autonomy of art reflects man's moral self-determination becomes almost absolute among Kant's immediate followers. They identify it with human freedom in history, which embodies the principle as an endless manifestation of will and consciousness. The complementary activity of the Ego—the shaping principle—is made synonymous with the highest ideals of action in history as well as in art. Creative genius is thought to solve artistic problems by confronting the infinite opposition between conscious and unconscious forces with a special knowledge of the beautiful and the sublime—infinite in itself. For Schelling art is the highest union of freedom and necessity. Fichte identifies the creative Ego with the All; his pantheism supposes that nature's task is to reveal the potentiality of the ideal in the real. Nature is concerned with potential power; but man, who takes his whole being from God (and without whom God would not exist) is the only creature who is free or capable of freedom; so that, if nature's task is to express potencies, man's task is to create personalities.

It is easy to see how these assumptions about the self-determined nature of man lead to the two Romantic extremes of a superhuman heroism and a programmatic esthetic divorced from all ethical norms—subsequently so familiar in an art-for-art's sake doctrine. But these general, well-known consequences often obscure the eminence of Kant's case for the autonomy of art, which issues from his critical philosophy and theory of knowledge.

Since, according to Kant, everything we know and sense is shaped through the Ego and is based on a fund of real or possible experience, the traditional object-subject dichotomy which vexes all prior philosophic speculation loses its conditional emphasis. As a result art gains significance in being a higher activity than the general sort involved in any engagement between man and his surroundings. The stress upon the subjectivity of all experience implies the need for a consciousness open to everything, experience itself being linked with the pure reason. Thus all man's faculties have their importance, including the imagination. We know the sublime, for instance, through our feelings: a stormy sea is not sublime but rather the feelings which the sight of it excites in the mind and which lead us to ideas of higher adaptation. Unlike Plato and Aristotle, Kant does not say that the important thing is nature as the symbol of God's capacity, but the capacity in the individual man to discern the beautiful and to introduce the sublime into the idea of nature.

The tragic tension between man's fate as a sensuous being and his adaptive capacities as an intelligible being also becomes apparent through such confrontations with the power of nature. For that which makes us fearful as sensuous beings, as, say, the stormy sea, at the same time activates in us a force which does not belong to nature. In the light of this force what we fear becomes trivial, and we are made independent of nature and its power, and able to exist in accord with our own individual destinies.

Art as an autonomous creation, the product of man's will and consciousness, bears the mark of certain a priori judgments of necessity and strict universality. Such usage of the a priori judgment is deeply related, for Kant, to the morally good—his one categorical imperative—so that esthetic taste is a "faculty" which judges ethical ideas in their sensible manifestations. This view disengages art from the regulative rule of moral prescription. Since the work of art has evolved its own regulations, we must think of it as a symbolic construction creating the sensible form of the ideal (Kant's morally good) rather than merely reflecting or translating some predetermined morality.

In applying Kant's theories to a metaphysics of the imagination, Romantic criticism is symbolic and psychological at its best. But it also tends to hedge over questions of form and expression, being more careful about making philosophic distinctions than of formulating its own principles.

The best example of this is Coleridge, whose criticism towers over that of his contemporaries because of his comprehensive interests and because of the insights he brings, from many other fields, to basic literary problems. As a principal source of the modern opposition to the concept of allegory, he is probably responsible—because his strictures on the subject have been taken too literally or misapplied—for instigating numerous pedantic distinctions between symbolism and allegory. Much of the notorious disorientation of Coleridge's criticism is due to the half-fought defensive campaigns he undertook on behalf of a new literature that had not fully come into existence and against the vested interest of ultrarational literary proprieties which had denied Elizabethan and Jacobean writers their due. It is in this context—particularly in the *Shakespeare Lectures* (1818)—that his well-known statement on mechanic and organic forms occurs; and this statement voices his basic attitude toward a similar distinction, made subsequently, between two kinds of trope.

The form is mechanic when on any given material we impress a predetermined form, not necessarily arising out of the properties of the material;—as when to a mass of wet clay we give whatever shape we wish it to retain when hardened. The organic form, on the other hand, is innate; it shapes, as it develops, itself from within, and the fulness of its development is one and the same with the perfection of its outward form. Such as the life is, such is the form.

The distinction echoes Aristotle's separation of "extrinsic" and "intrinsic" causes, as well as the ancient notion that all art has the unity of a living creature. Yet the point of Coleridge's comparison seems singularly unconvincing because, under the pressures of definition, he raises two interrelated kinds of artistic approach and effect to the level of antagonistic principles. Concerning mechanic form we must imagine that the shape given "a mass of wet clay" is impressed from outside, as by a potter, while the innate "organic form" necessarily evolves from within, according to some unspeakable process of self-determination. The innate "life" of the organic form suggests an embryo visibly growing into adult form, while the view of the mechanic form—which is "pre-determined"—implies little more than the potter's gross need to sell pots. The odds are plainly stacked on the side of organic form against the patent fact that all art working in many directions toward its fulfillment invariably and simultaneously depends upon both types of "form." Further observations, in *Miscellaneous Criticism* and *Anima Poetae*, make explicit Coleridge's notion of allegory, and reflect the prejudice and fascination shown by the most sensitive critics writing on the subject.

In the first statement his prescription for "allegoric writing" is disguised as a definition:

We may thus safely define allegoric writing as the employment of one set of agents and images with actions and accompaniments correspondent, so as to convey, while in disguise, either moral qualities or conceptions of the mind that are not in themselves objects of the senses, or other images, agents, actions, fortunes, and circumstances, so that the difference is everywhere presented to the idea or imagination while the likeness is suggested to the mind; and this connectedly so that the parts combine to form a consistent whole.[13]

Like his remarks on organic and mechanical form, the definition rehearses common rhetorical notions in order to stress an underlying esthetic idea which favors the symbolic over the allegorical procedure. These notions are implied in his opposing moral qualities to sensuous imagery, in his emphasizing the "disguise" of one object as another, and in his characterizing the metaphoric essence in allegory as a presentation of a difference in a likeness. Coleridge's last clause, on the connectedness of the parts to the whole, merely states a general principle that might be applied to any writing whatever. Looked at more closely, however, the statement tells us that allegorical writing is equivalent to a stylistic *tour de force,* mechanically worked out like a sleight-of-hand trick. At the end, he remarks that all "this" (trickery?) in its "parts" should somehow "combine" into "a consistent whole." This attitude reappears in *Miscellaneous Criticism* when Coleridge distinguishes the Symbolical from the Allegorical:

The Symbolical cannot, perhaps, be better defined in distinction from the Allegorical, than that it is always itself a part of that, of the whole of which it is representative.—"Here comes a sail,"—(that is, a ship) is a symbolical expression. "Behold our lion!" when we speak of some gallant soldier, is allegorical. Of most importance to our present subject is this point, that the latter (the allegory) cannot be other than spoken consciously;—whereas in the former (the symbol) it is very possible that the general truth may be unconsciously in the writer's mind during the construction of the symbol; and it proves itself by being produced out of his own mind,—as the Don Quixote out of the perfectly sane mind of Cervantes, and not by outward observation, or historically. The advantage of symbolic writing over allegory is, that it presumes no disjunction of faculties, but simple predominance.[14]

Taken in themselves, these distinctions between allegory and symbolism serve as a convenience in the interests of definition-making. The uncertain, pedantic style gives some indication of this: an effluence of doubt rising from the qualifying words, "perhaps" and "may be" and "presume" and "very possible." Actually the definitions are only variations on the stock distinction between synecdoche and metonymy. Even if this separating of the Symbolical and the Allegorical were more than a grammatical quibble over similar functions of the tropes, one would still have to show how either trope prevails throughout such an extended work as *Don Quixote.*

Coleridge's idea of the way symbolism works includes the notion of a general truth concealed in the writer's unconscious mind, having its origin there and growing spontaneously into the fictional work. But this view illustrates Coleridge's principle of organic form better than it does the symbolical principle. From it we deduce that in being "explicit" or denotative allegory suffers the fate of the pot in the potter's hands—its form must be imposed from the outside, "consciously." Hence allegory must be taken as a specimen of mechanical, and not of organic, form. Symbolic writing is esthetically more satisfying than allegorical writing because "it presumes no disjunction of faculties"—that is, no separation between mind and imagination, or conscious and unconscious processes.

Another remark, from *Anima Poetae*, indicates the significant philosophic bias underlying Coleridge's view of symbolic creation:

In looking at objects of Nature I seem rather to be seeking, as it were *asking* for, a symbolical language for something within me that already and for ever exists, than observing anything new.

This view of symbolic language anticipates the typical inward regard of the later symbolists—as it is echoed, for example, in Baudelaire's sonnet *Correspondances*—identifying the aim of art with the artist's conscientious expression of personality rather than with the mimetic principle of art as an imitation of nature and life.

And so if we take Coleridge's strictures on allegory literally, as most modern critics do, we find a case against the concept of a devalued sort of metaphor-making in poetry and fiction. The same argument serves axiomatically to support the case for symbolism. It is probably not a vital part of the issue that Coleridge scarcely amplifies his view beyond making negative references to the allegory in *The Pilgrim's Progress, The Faerie Queene*, and Dante's *Commedia*, or that he pays much more attention to works representing the symbolic principle, as his studies of Shakespeare and Cervantes show. But we do risk missing his main reason for setting up the symbol-vs.-allegory distinction if we fail to see it within the perspective of his general criticism and his philosophy of the imagination.

His urgent need to propagandize the cause of the imagination shows up in the thin slicing of his case, the pseudo definition-making, and the application of Kantian metaphysics to all questions involving metaphoric language. His more detailed inquiries into the faculties of imagination and fancy, together with the passages on mechanic and organic form, are aggressive attempts to substantiate his own literary philosophy in its extension from Kant's ethical principles and Hartley's associational psychology. This is everywhere apparent in the *Biographia Literaria* and *Lectures* where Coleridge cites the effects of connecting just taste and pure morality in art as being the creation of an organic unity. For poetry, he says in the *Shakespeare Lectures,* "like all other living powers, must of necessity circumscribe itself by rules, were it only to unite power with beauty; it must embody itself to reveal itself; but a living body is of necessity an organized one. . . ." He writes similarly in the *Biographia* (XIV) of the "synthetic and magical power" of the imagination:

This power . . . reveals itself in the balance and reconcilement of opposite or discordant qualities; of sameness, with difference; of the general with the concrete; the idea with the image; the individual with the representative; . . . while it . . . harmonizes the natural and the artificial, still subordinates art to nature; the manner to the matter. . . .

The "esemplastic" process, where the thinking subject coalesces with the object, is a function of the primary imagination—"the living power and prime agent of the eternal act of creation in the infinite I AM." But the wedge which Coleridge drives between imagination and fancy serves not only to differentiate a creative from a merely reproductive capacity of mind, but also to convert what usage had regarded as one thing into two kinds of poetry. Like Kant, Coleridge is opposed to a priori accounts of the dualism involving subject-object relationship in medieval and classical philosophy. For him the creative imagination itself becomes a faith, a pure morality without the restrictions of legalistic dogma. In Shakespeare's Ariel he finds that "what is called poetic faith is required and created, and our common notions of philosophy give way before it: this feeling may be said to be much stronger than historic faith, since for the exercise of poetic faith the mind is previously prepared." [15] If we make the connection implied by his distinctions, allegory may be seen to share the qualities of fancy and simile—that is, in being limited as both are to merely decorative or univocal inventions, it brings "together images dissimilar in the main by some one point or more of likeness"; and being likewise limited, as fancy is, it represents only "a mode of memory" that plays with "fixities and definites." [16]

In seeking an absolute conjunction between mind and nature, intuitive and empirical knowledge, form and matter in art, Coleridge, like most Romantics, finds that the known values of experience are best expressed through the predilections of a transcendental personal ego. This opinion is not opposed to the medieval belief in the formal and functional truth of objective reality. It reformulates the medieval belief with a different emphasis, giving it, as it were, a centripetal instead of a centrifugal direction. Presumably, however, the medieval writer did not have to challenge the phenomenal world of his immediate perception. Ideally he did not have to ask, as Coleridge did, for a symbolic language outside himself to confirm something that existed inside himself. The symbolic language was prescribed from the start in the supposition that God's world exists as a comprehensive creation, a creation in which the perceiver and the thing perceived are similar events. Coleridge assumes the same philosophic split which confronted the early Church fathers, and which, by means of Christian analogy, was later resolved in dogma—the split, that is, between subject and object, between the language of the inward eye and the language of nature. But Coleridge goes on to show how they are merged and reconciled by the creative imagination, not by an a priori rationale based on dogmatics. Given this emphasis we see why

Coleridge turns against the traditional concept of allegory and towards a refurbished concept of symbolism.

5. *The Object Rediscovered: Signifying the Irrational*

After Coleridge, Romantic doctrine urges the dominance of art over nature; artistic imagination alone may prescribe and encompass all value in a world of indeterminate orders and conflicting energies. The extreme of this doctrine suggests that anything may be called art if the imagination so decrees. Accordingly, if nature has any meaning at all, it is because man chooses to recognize or use it, and not because of the functions assigned to it by the Godhead or by Bacon, Newton, and Locke. The Romantic view is mainly symbolic but its notion of symbolism is diffuse, limited, and often arbitrary, depending upon the artist's expressive originality rather than his perceptive integrity. In French symbolism and in nonobjective esthetics, the fragmentary insight, the musical pattern, or the verbal arrangement is deliberately set forth as the *ne plus ultra* against the impossibility of creating an ordered vision of the whole in any terms. Little or no relationship is conceivable between nature and the created work of art. Yet every art is compounded of natural forms, the shape and action of phenomenal objects, events, and personalities. To reject this fact and the implications to be drawn from it is to disable the expressive possibilities of art. The programmatic denial of a subject-object relationship leads to the devaluation of art, converting the art product into an artifact having only the most spurious meaning for the maker and the beholder. Ultimately this attitude invites the sterility of virtuoso performance, academicism, and esthetic cultism at their worst.

But though the articulation of this extreme view may be traced to Coleridge and the Romantics generally, it would be foolish to blame them for its consequences. The inveterate habitué of impasses is not necessarily the creator of impasses; he may simply be quicker than others to sense and explore them. In this way the Romantic was often the discoverer of an existential reality that went beyond the illusory subjectivism and a laissez-faire morality inherited from an iconoclastic Protestantism. The fault with the Romantic's successor, the art-for-art's saker, the esthetic extremist, is that he is content to take the impasses for granted, and to proceed as if no other way existed or might possibly be found. In maintaining this crucial disparity between an impossibly complex universe outside himself, and the order his ego discovers in art, the Romantic extremist summarily dismisses the external world. But it is actually he himself, in consequence of his dislocated view, who dwindles in effectiveness and capacity as a creator.

Subsequently, the animus against allegory comes to be propagated by no one so much as the symbolist-in-retreat.[17] Melville, for instance, denies the allegory in *Moby Dick*, although there must have been something in Hawthorne's lost letter that convinced him he had used it in a new way since he was later able to accept the "part-&-parcel allegoricalness of the whole." [18] In Coleridge there is something almost flippant, a note of having conjectured vainly for too long, which one senses in his heads-I-win-tails-you-lose argument: ". . . if the allegoric personage be strongly individualized so as to interest us, we cease to think of it as allegory; and if it does not interest us, it had better be away." [19] Poe, on reading Hawthorne's *Tales*, echoes Coleridge's dismissal of allegory as a useless game: "The deepest allegory, *as* allegory, is a very, very imperfectly satisfied sense of the writer's ingenuity in overcoming a difficulty we should have preferred his not having attempted to overcome."[20] Presumably there can be nothing serious or problematic about allegory since it appeals only to the fanciful side of the imagination. Thus Henry James reminds one of Coleridge and Poe when he remarks about Hawthorne,

. . . allegory to my sense is quite one of the lighter exercises of the imagination. Many excellent judges, I know, have a great stomach for it; they delight in symbols and correspondences, in seeing a story told as if it were another and a very different story. I frankly confess that I have as a general thing but little enjoyment of it, and that it has never seemed to me to be, as it were, a first-rate literary form. . . . It is apt to spoil two good things—a story and a moral, a meaning and a form; and the taste for it is responsible for a large part of the forcible-feeble writing that has been inflicted upon the world.[21]

In opposing allegory as didactic personification, these writers are undoubtedly measuring their distance from such popular examples as Bunyan's *Holy War* and *The Pilgrim's Progress*. When a simple moralism, a confectionery kind of Romanticism, or a strong naturalistic bias invades novelistic fiction, writers and critics may use the term symbolism to indicate an area of fictional practice that is at least immune from subliterary contagions. Still, the fictions of Melville, Poe, Hawthorne, and James, like the narrative poems of Coleridge, often hide behind the fanciful, even when they are most serious.[22] Generally in their work the qualities of elusiveness and understatement, of mystification and wit, expressed in an excruciating tone of lightness that pretends to a salutary suppression of the horrible and irrational, make for a growing tension that ultimately reveals the dead-seriousness behind the make-believe. Such equivocations unite these writers on a common ground of symbolic intent, and attract the reader who sees in them an essentially symbolic or allegorical approach.

New England transcendentalism managed to sustain a moral vision which was most fruitful for allegory. Nineteenth-century American fiction satirized extreme Romanticism as well as overoptimistic liberalism. It often looked ironically at an iconoclastic realism and an overrationalized determinism. A new sensitivity to psychological motives and a growing suspicion of a superindividualistic ethics began to indicate how the glorification of the irrational led to hypocrisy or self-destruction. But the irrational had somehow to be accounted for—the sense of being fascinated by it as well as the sense of being repelled by it. And this ambivalence in attitude toward the irrational is typically suited to the method and purpose of allegory.

From the beginning, allegory has offered the rational consciousness a way of regulating imaginative materials that otherwise appear confounded by contradictions and bristling with destructive implications. In allegory the irrational becomes viable through a corporative method that may be called differentiation: the narrative builds up the sense of the distinctions to be drawn among the "levels of meaning" and between the accidental and the purposeful, the explicit and the implicit, and so on. The irrational is thereby given an authentic, undiminished force which otherwise—according to law, custom, dogma—would be distorted or obscured. This constant layering of meaning in the narrative proves to be decisive in creating the whole effect which the literary work can have upon us. When one thinks of the great mythopoeic works like the Bible, *Oedipus Rex*, and the Homeric poems, harnessed as they have been by extensive commentary, it is striking that the interpreters have focused their efforts on domesticating the irregular and forbidding insights which, if taken literally, would be destructive of the very code on which society is built.

Among the modern critics Kenneth Burke, for one, has been especially concerned with the reciprocal workings of social and esthetic phenomena. Since philosophical thought is often "a translation of narrative terms into 'timeless' ones," he reminds us that the early poetic "ways of essentializing in terms of act and image eventually became transformed into the high generalizations of philosophy." Once laws and principles are fixed philosophically, however, the matter is usually turned around, so that "whereas the philosophic expressions were later translations of the earlier narrative ones, we may look upon narrative expressions as translations of philosophic ones." [23]

As we have seen, it is this translative use of narrative method and cultural ideal which characterizes the concept of allegory —a particular kind of thinking in myth, literature, and philoso-

phy whose purpose (to preserve an old truth, to renew a forgotten one) requires translation. There are all sorts of translation, however. And there is an obvious difference between the
slavish translation which misses the point of the original and
the inspired translation which may even improve upon the
original. The difference is between a mere rendering and a
thorough re-creation in another form. What, for instance, is
good doctrine to philosophers or theologians may be only a
stimulating idea to a poet, or even a complete redundancy. And,
although the poet may simply have adapted the idea for his
own use, an entire tradition of criticism thereafter tries to determine what the poet meant by a Beatrice or a Hamlet, taking
pains to distinguish the imaginary characters and events from
the historical ones, as if that were the only way of coming
upon the answer. The inspired kind of translative thinking succeeds in recasting an outworn original—as Sophocles recast the
Greek theogony or as Dante recast the system of Christian
analogy—in a new organic structure which provides more vital
means for the narrative expression of those who follow.

The main vehicles used for conveying material between
speculative thought and imaginative literature are the figurative elements of metaphor, irony, symbol, and allegory. Allegory, as we have seen, serves more comprehensively than the
other tropes in structuring the design of a fiction. Being more
schematic and more flexible than is usually supposed, allegory
is also the literary type that engages, more fully than any other,
the symbolic uses of literature. The implications of such uses,
like those involving the commerce between literature and ideas,
lead into an area where the practices of allegory must be seen
in a wider perspective to include the workings of epic, satire,
and pastoral. The interconnections between each of these
types and the particular ideal it is created to express will be discussed in a later chapter. It should be apparent by then that
the good or the bad reputation of symbolic fictions, so often
based on some assumption about the writer's philosophical
biases or borrowings, in no way relates to the practical matters
of his fulfilling his literary aims and methods in the fiction.

III

Construction

Two things of opposite natures seem to depend
On one another, as a man depends
On a woman, day on night, the imagined

On the real. This is the origin of change.
Winter and spring, cold copulars, embrace
And forth the particulars of rapture come.

Music falls on the silence like a sense,
A passion that we feel, not understand.
Morning and afternoon are clasped together

And North and South are an intrinsic couple
And sun and rain a plural, like two lovers
That walk away as one in the greenest body.

In solitude the trumpets of solitude
Are not of another solitude resounding;
A little string speaks for a crowd of voices.

The partaker partakes of that which changes him.
The child that touches takes character from the thing,
The body, it touches. The captain and his men

Are one and the sailor and the sea are one.
Follow after, O my companion, my fellow, my self,
Sister and solace, brother and delight.

WALLACE STEVENS, *Notes toward a Supreme Fiction*

1. Polarities: The Metamorphosis of Opposites

ALLEGORICAL fictions from Dante to Kafka have much more in common with one another than with other kinds of fiction written by contemporaries in the respective periods. For allegories, of whatever period, dramatize similar ideals and problems concerning the nature of man. They employ myths and archetypes symbolically in a portrayal of human wishes and defeats. These characteristics are fundamentally related to the process of rationalizing mythical materials in a dogma or religious text. And so to get at the typical form of allegorical fictions, one may well start with the foremost of rationalized mysteries: the allegory of the creation in the Bible.

Genesis presents the creation out of chaos as a separation between light and darkness after light has been evoked.

> In the beginning God created the heaven and the earth. And the earth was without form, and void; and darkness was upon the face of the deep. And God said, Let there be light: and there was light. And God saw the light, that it was good: and God divided the light from the darkness. And God called the light Day, and the darkness he called Night. And the evening and the morning were the first day. (I, 1–5)

The Gospel of St. John interprets the creation intellectually as the revelation of the Logos, the Will or Word of the Creator inseparable from its embodiment in the Creator.

> In the beginning was the Word, and the Word was with God, and the Word was God. The same was in the beginning with God. All things were made by him; and without him was not any thing made that was made. In him was life; and the life was the light of men. And the light shineth in darkness; and the darkness comprehendeth it not. (I, 1–5)

57

The beginning according to Genesis concerns the literal creation of the world by a single being who sets up, then distinguishes between, the most fundamental of natural oppositions:
day and night. Although looking back to the creation story in
Genesis as an historical event, the beginning according to St.
John provides little that can be understood as original creation.
In St. John the Creator is the principle of life and a symbol, "the
light of men." Darkness, physically and intellectually opposed
to light, surrounds the principle and the symbol. St. John interprets the adjective "good" from Genesis—where it means something like "satisfactory"—to suggest moral enlightenment. Similarly, in the succeeding verses of St. John, light becomes the
"true Light," meaning Christ or "the Word made flesh."

Thus, to be understood comprehensively, the Gospel description must be taken as a spiritual fulfillment of the figure set
forth in Genesis. Nor does the comprehensive meaning of
Christ's life become understandable until the Gospel account
of it is taken as a spiritual fulfillment of the figurative representation which appears in the Genesis story of the Fall.[1] St. John's
emphasis on the authority of the Word—derived from the will
of the Creator and incarnated in the world He creates, that is,
no longer separate from God, as the created world is in Genesis
—becomes the doctrinal model for all Christian allegories.

Nothing better illustrates the way in which an allegorical interpretation of a fiction consumes and supersedes the fiction
itself by adapting fundamental natural oppositions from one
text and amplifying them in another. Moreover, the relationship between Genesis and St. John indicates how one myth de-
pendent upon an earlier one for its authority is turned into a
mystery. God's creative work in Genesis becomes His Word in
the Gospel; and the Fall of man through his disobedience is
converted into the deliberate penance of Christ on the Cross,
His death and resurrection for the salvation of mankind. The
original event generates the Word, which in turn comprises a
new event—the life of Christ. The life of Christ then encompasses all antecedent (anticipatory) events in Genesis, to be-

come the Word fulfilled, which, in the form of a mystic dogma, regulates man's understanding of the creation story. The original, partly rationalized creation story in Genesis thus loses its mythical character on being reshaped into a rationally determined mystery in the Gospel.

The license for such interpretative transfiguration is supplied by the medieval analogical system, which sought to preserve Christian dogma both historically and eternally on rational grounds. In Thomas Aquinas' summary, the "divine science" of Christian analogy significantly assumes the intelligibility of God's Word as a first principle (since God the Creator is also "the author" of the Scriptures), thereby enabling one systematically "to read" His cosmic intention (His will) in words that relate to things as well as in things themselves.

The author of Holy Writ is God, in whose power it is to signify His meaning, not by words only (as man also can do), but also by things themselves. So, whereas in every other science things are signified by words, this science has the property, that the things signified by the words have themselves also a signification. Therefore that first signification whereby words signify things belongs to the first sense, the historical or literal. That signification whereby things signified by words have themselves also a signification is called the spiritual sense, which is based on the literal, and presupposes it. (*Summa,* I. Q. I, Art. 10)

The threefold division of the spiritual sense is distinguished as allegorical, moral, and anagogical. Each differs from the literal sense in function, but all three depend upon it, as upon a basic structure, for their spiritual truth. The corporative sense is what Christian analogy finds in the literal sense so that, first, the meaning of things existing historically and objectively may be made manifest; and, secondly, that such meaning may be shown to have been inherent (presupposed) in the literal event from the beginning—through the Word of God.

The symbolic distinction here—on a metaphoric basis, of a difference in a likeness, and a likeness in a difference—is part of a conceptual construction founded on the dualistic implications of the Creation and the Fall in Genesis. In this analogical determination of the bases of contiguity between the historical and the eternal, between things signified by words and the signification of things signified by words, one can see a revealing similarity to the hypothetical relationship between creative design generally—purpose as well as form—and all narration. For what Aquinas regards as the literal or historical sense is not substantially different from what custom regards as the fictional basis of a narrative. Certainly it is the sense least amenable to being tampered with by the critical interpreter.[2] A fiction (novel, play, narrative poem) bears somewhat the same relation to reality—any sequential organization of facts based on observation or experience—as the literal sense, according to Aquinas, bears to the spiritual. When we say that a fiction objectifies reality, we mean that it makes the real world more or less palatable for us. At the same time, the fictional delineation corresponds to two fundamental truths about the nature of experience. Simply by existing around us, the world requires to be interpreted and understood; and whatever the interpretation, it assumes initially a dualistic or parallel relationship (e.g., mind and body, object and subject, idea and thing) concerning the nature of reality. And this quite aside from any moral implications about the meaning of the relationship.

Given such needs coincident with human consciousness, which in itself bears the dualistic inclination, the artist or interpreter welds two separate events together in order to incorporate an earlier "literal" within a later "spiritual" signification. In this way the artist-interpreter presumably makes whole again what conscious man at first saw as unrelated experiences. Basically such experiences may only have been man's sense of himself as against everything not himself. As such they necessarily would serve to make him aware of the possibilities of developing or using the world around him. The creative mind attempts, as it were, to heal the wound made by separation from the matrix of the world around it. Man's consciousness in-flicts the wound and his creative mind tries to heal it when he distinguishes the nature of the world from which he has issued and within which he must work. (Or, as this phenomenon is reflected in the scientific method, the data must first be identi-fied and distinguished before they are realistically grouped to-gether.)

The axiomatic system upon which Christian dogma relies, rises from an interpretative method that confronts and inter-relates one fiction with another. If, as Aquinas put it, "the Old Law is a figure of the New Law," and "the New Law itself is a figure of future glory," then neither fiction (Old or New) can be understood apart from the other. Interpretative genius has driven the two fictions so firmly together that they have actually become inseparable, except for non-Christians.

To summarize: how this union of two texts is achieved de-pends upon the value given the symbol in Aquinas' analogi-cal prescription. The thing represented by the symbolic word is itself symbolic of God's meaning. Hence in any context it be-comes possible to specify the doctrinal senses according to the double semantic function of the word, which points backward and forward at the same time. Yet the primary function of the analogical or of any symbolic system is not properly to get at a philosophical truth but to employ the symbol in its simultane-ous progressive and retrogressive direction, thereby making history and experience meaningful. When we ask that a fiction be verisimilar, that it accord with some notion of how things "really are," we are not asking to be told a philosophical truth either. We are asking for what is hypothetically or ideally "prob-able"—which is usually why we go to fiction (a pleasant de-lusion, as it is called) to look for it in the first place. It is only when we mistake the fiction for "real" life, or the "letter" (in *literal*-minded fashion) for "the truth of the matter," and fol-low it like a recipe, that we risk becoming Don Quixotes. And yet it is precisely by grappling with "fictional" relationships of this sort—as *Don Quixote* indeed shows—where opposites have dramatic functions that distinctions between the real and the probable become significant to us.

Oppositional relationships in allegory often follow the example of Biblical interpretation, where figurations based on original polarities are related to objects, events, and persons having specific identities. This device is fruitful, since it may be used again and again to extend or convert fictional identities. The original polarities of darkness and light, night and day, death and life, define the extent of the cosmos, the arena of human action and thought. By means of such oppositions all of life may be represented accordingly. Considered diagrammatically, the cosmos is a circle; intersecting diameters stand for opposite levels or directions of earthly and spiritual aspirations. On the same circular ground one may imagine the work of creation. Here the seven days correspond to a geocentric view of the universe: the earth in the center is surrounded at various points on the perimeter by the sun, moon, and five planets. This cosmic structure suggests human and moral counterparts into which it may be translated. The revolution of the stars and the natural cycle of days and seasons correspond to the human cycle of generation, death, and resurrection. They are also analogous to the growth and decline of the living consciousness in the individual life. In religious contexts the intersecting diameters form a cross, which signifies all the physical and psychic dualities projected by man. By taking the temporal dimension as the horizontal line, and the spatial dimension as the vertical line, the extreme points of the one will mark the extent of corporeal existence, and the extreme points of the other will mark the extent of spiritual existence. The lines may further signify the planes of infinity and eternity, the extremes of consciousness and unconsciousness, and so forth.

In allegory the original polarities, whose myriad relationships and parallels are illustrated by the cross within the circle, may be extended or converted to fit the requirements of any narrative. Dante and the Italian Neoplatonists, for instance, extend the dichotomy of day and night to indicate the difference between wakefulness and sleep; their meaning is that people concerned with divine things are awake while all others are asleep or merely dreaming. Or the struggle of good and evil may be shown by the powers of white and black magic in complementary agents. The sense of the meaning of the struggle between such powers helps to create character and to advance narrative action. Fundamental polarities gradually gather to themselves clusters of parallel oppositions, so that on one level dark and light are synonymous, say, with animal and human, lust and love; on another level, with seeming and being, mutability and permanence; on still another level, with doubt and will, despair and faith. But obviously these polarities can express no degree of real urgency without a specific fictional embodiment.

In Book One of *The Faerie Queene* the relationship between characters continually shifts, although they preserve their parallel identities in fixed opposition to one another. The figure of Una is a good example. She is generally related to the Red Cross Knight, who serves her, as Truth to Holiness; but by the same virtue, she is progressively set against Duessa, Archimago, Sansloy, Sansfoy, and Sansjoy—the figures of deception and faithlessness actively opposing her. She also appears in various guises, as the embodiment of the Virgin, Elizabeth the Queen, Chaste Love, and the True (Protestant) Church. These identities become clear as the action successively focuses on her happy juxtaposition or her perilous opposition with other figures. Consequently, even when standing alone she can be seen either as Truth without Holiness or as the totality of all her roles momentarily held together and waiting to be summoned into action. At one such point she is accompanied by a lion, symbolic of British policy and royal prerogative, and this particularization extends her role once again. The auxiliary figure of the lion, who never reappears, reveals a latent aspect of her total character.

Or take the example of Kafka's *Metamorphosis*. The structure of oppositional relationships is not more complex than in *The Faerie Queene*. It is conditioned differently; that is, by a realistic milieu instead of a mythicized fairyland. Yet Kafka's localization is significantly deceptive, for it is really an emanation of the hero's own disabled consciousness. Only through this inward focus are the scene and characters realized, although the objective tone of the narrative, emphasizing the exigent event and the action of others, makes the focus and relationship appear to be outward.

Like Spenser's Knights of Holiness and Temperance, who are designated in their missions at the start, Kafka's Gregor Samsa has already been judged when the story begins. That judgment and the self-punishment it entails are the conditions the story undertakes to dramatize. In Spenser the relationship of man to society is partly established in the feudal obligations of the knights to their queen, and partly in the Christian nature of their missions, where the particular virtue they enact is manifested. In *The Metamorphosis* this relationship, always at stake and continually being questioned, is reduced to one concerning a man and his immediate family. Authority rests with the father and the social injunction to work, which he represents. (In *The Castle* Kafka asks, "Does not the least degree of authority contain the whole?") Gregor's "crime"—his sudden and inexplicable inertia—immediately causes his metamorphosis. From a state of social and filial obligation, centered in his work as the family's indefatigable breadwinner, he falls into an animal-like lethargy—i.e., he lies down on the job. From the beginning, then, it is both his punishment and the means of his *éclaircissement* to contend with himself and others as a giant insect equipped with human consciousness.

The darkness out of which Gregor emerges transformed is on one level the darkness of a former life, a guilty sleep—the sleep of an impossibly routinized and self-alienated existence. The life to which he wakes when the story opens is the frightening life of new awareness. He has dreamed himself, perhaps unconsciously wished himself, completely out of social usefulness. Of course, as it soon becomes clear, he has wished himself out of the sort of social usefulness imposed upon him without his conscious assent—without his having been permitted to choose the kind of work which would be both possible and right for him. His dilemma is that he must challenge, grapple with, and seek protection from the judgment that society places on him for deserting his work, and at the same time accept the judgment, the guilt he actually feels, "lying down." On this level, the physical equivalent of the social and psychological metamorphosis—and the overt sign of his rebellion and ostracism—is what he becomes to his family and to himself as he lies in bed: simply a huge, detestable insect.

Precisely because his metamorphosis is so unmistakable, Gregor can now summon his past life into consciousness. Abandoned to animal abjectness and mere spectatorship, he begins to understand the "human" condition as he represents it. And since his separation from the family has been made manifest, he can now try to come to terms with his alienated condition and his inarticulate yearnings. We are gradually made to see him, almost literally in the mosaic vision of an insect, reflecting the totality of many fragmentary bits of behavior toward him on the part of his office superior, his sister, his mother, his father, the family boarders, and finally the charlady. As he is seen by each in turn, there is a cumulative and recapitulative sense which confirms his physical metamorphosis. The effect is simultaneously to strip down to its essential absurdity the inadequacy of their responses as well as to exhibit him becoming exactly what each takes him for.

To his sister, who seems closest to him, he is most unequivocally understood in his animal needs. She brings him the garbage he relishes and battens on. To his office superior, the chief clerk, he is that unheard-of monster who broke the rule of punctuality—even so, the most negligible of all the impossibly stringent rules of office routine. The father, whose complete lack of self-discipline makes him lean on others, exaggerates the authority he does not use on himself, so that when imposed on others it becomes a terrible virtue covering and compensating for his own defects. Thus when Gregor's father beats him back with a stick and hysterically pelts him with apples, Gregor encounters the punishment by which a purblind authority asserts itself and grows strong. And, as a result of Gregor's metamorphosis, his father, formerly a sick, useless old man, turns into a vigorous job-holding bank official. When Gregor's metamorphosis is accepted as a fact, the other characters show themselves for what they are. The mother is without real understanding in her compassion. The intrusive boarders insultingly evaluate the situation, and this in turn calls forth the wrath of the father, who in driving them out of the house unifies the family against Gregor. It is as though the family needed first to have the goad of the boarders' social disapprobation in order to swallow its own distaste and personal chagrin, before finally expressing its own real feelings overtly. At the end, the charlady, moved by malice, prods Gregor's dying body with a broom; having no organized system of "values" to propel her upward, she can only demonstrate her frustrations in such forms of gratuitous revenge.

The metamorphosis which started within the hero's consciousness earlier now becomes the gross outward fact of his physical transformation. This exposure of an exaggerated debasement gradually provokes a series of reactions among successive characters, who thereby assist in dramatizing the hero's identity. The identification proceeds step by step, and at each development we see how the central metaphor (metamorphosis) relates to, and finally overwhelms, the hero's awareness.

Answering Gregor's need for love and understanding there is shame, expressed by his sister's covert recognition of his animal needs, while his mother can only grieve mutely for the old Gregor, whom she pictures in the illusory past he has discarded. Repudiating Gregor's anxious industry and personal merit as a jobholder is the machinery of institutionalized legalities represented by the chief clerk. In response to Gregor's need for guidance and support is the rivalry of the father and the authoritarian justice he wrathfully voices. Gregor's situation is a limbo where the forces of oppositional entities—dark-light, animal-human, lust-love, seeming-being, despair-faith—are constantly refracted through his consciousness and exposed in his immediate surroundings. Since he cannot assert any actual sense of himself, he falls prey to those forces in himself and in others that have hopelessly mistaken him. It is as if he negatively and inevitably "self-awares" himself out of existence on learning how arbitrary his identity is; or how, in depending so largely on others, it must perish for lack of the right sustenance. If the social dispensation, typified by the self-preservation of the family, is pre-eminent, who then is the individual alone? The story seems to answer the question by ironically posing another: Nobody?

And yet, as seen through the dramatization of his needs and failures, Gregor's identity and the problematic issue it raises are developed in the distorted relationship between himself and others, which he has permitted or encouraged to grow. This may be put in the form of another question: What has he actually given of himself that he should expect others, with similar needs, to give something in return? In such terms, the final criticism seems not to be leveled against society so much as against Gregor, who sinks into his dilemma because he is unable to find his real self. The fact that each character in the story may be taken as a personification of some particular defect, essentially related to Gregor's instigative needs, becomes the core of the criticism. All the characters thereby show their own deadly stultification, including Gregor in his bug-like form —the last degree of the process.

What Gregor reveals of himself through others, in their particular attributes, accounts for the outward direction of the allegory from an inward focus. This reverses the process in traditional allegory, which starts with the personified attribute, and by lending it urgency and vitality works inward to the meaning of the attribute in a pre-established moral context. In Kafka everything seems to proceed from the hero's self-judgment at the beginning. He has no vital mission; he has cut himself off from society. Thus, instead of extending his identity, like Una or Red Cross, by active juxtaposition and opposition to others, he constantly dwindles. He is seen, as it were, from the opposite end of the telescope: instead of finding his many actual identities, he shrinks and is finally converted into nothingness.

There is no moral closure in *The Metamorphosis*. It ends with the stark critical question of the individual and society which Gregor's metamorphosis poses. Earnest moralists will of course add what is lacking in the context—that a complete recognition of stultification, the full awareness of guilt or sin or dread, is the abyss of despair, and that its convincing portrayal is enough to make clear the need of a "leap," as the Existentialists call it, to commitment.

2. Dream Artifice: The Familiar Unknown

In *The Metamorphosis* and the first book of *The Faerie Queene* the world of concentrated purpose takes on the apparently fixed but vagrant characteristics of a dream. Freed from pressures of strict chronology and verisimilitude, the unfolding of basic oppositions is unusually fluent and persuasive. This suggests that the traditional dream artifice in allegorical narratives disguises deliberate intention in the form of a mystery or seeming irrelevances; and this quality invariably invites interpretation.

Experience tells us that the same thing occurs when we dream. The overtly psychic rhythm in a dream accompanies an underlying physical rhythm. Together they are reflected in the dream narrative and imagery which proceed demonstratively according to their own laws. It is as if in violating temporal sequence and standard patterns of behavior, the dream were illustrating something unusually significant in a totally irrational but self-contained manner. The dream's appeal-for-interpretation, as instigated by all its fixed and vagrant characteristics, may be associated with various deterministic theories based on the dualistic nature of man—as, for instance, the view that in man there is a constant alternation and vying for supremacy between the animal and angelic parts of his nature. The same dream phenomenon may also be associated with the Kantian formula that explains the motivating elements in human nature as a combination of the effects of freedom and necessity. Like the dream in its interpretability, the formula assumes that man in all his actions is a self-contained, self-"purposed" being, a thing-in-itself.

Besides expressing everyone's personal experience, the dream bears the interpretative imprint of priest and witch doctor, whose revelations were manifested in rites before the advent of a written literature. Dream interpreters have been admired and feared for their ability to grapple with the mysteries of the unknown, and perhaps even more for the complex symbolism of language and artifact they have created in order to expound the meaning of dreams. As modern psychology has shown, the dream of priest, president, or citizen is a mirror of acutely socialized material which the individual psyche of the dreamer reduces to formal symbols. The modern commonplace that the irrationality of dreams has a meaning which the reason fears to admit is surely a version of the older belief that dreams speak the symbolic language of a super-intelligence communicating commands and cautions which the reason is unwise to dismiss.

Since dream imagery bathes in underlying conflicts, the dream makes oppositional relationships much more distinct for the individual while dreaming than they appear when he is awake. For example, an adult's dream will often recur to an experience of childhood: a terrifying set-to with human figures who at one moment are fearful ogres and then suddenly become all-powerful protectors and benefactors. This unrationalized view seems puzzling until the dreamer realizes that he himself has colored and "wish-fulfilled" his dream characters under stress of deep, often ambivalent personal emotions. The dreamer's feelings toward his monster-protector, like the actions of the allegorical hero, seek to pin down not the who-ness but the what-ness of the agent—that is, those typical, immediately familiar traits which make the mysterious agent an attractive or repulsive figure. The child, the adult dreamer, and the allegorical hero will each know, with uncanny certainty, just what to anticipate of the force confronting him. Symbolic literature draws upon these typical attributes of the dream and the individual dreamer's experience. In allegories which conventionalize it as a narrative device, the dream serves additional, often unsuspected ends.

As with the first words of fables—"in the beginning" or "once upon a time" or "long ago"—the dream artifice introduces a world with unspecified dimensions of time and space. In the cluttered playground of fantasy an arena of the absolute is suddenly disclosed where relationships between agents, agent and action, and action and purpose may be subtilized in ways that few other fictional artifices permit. Transcending customary qualifications, the introduction of the artifice immediately declares that moral identities—dream impulsions dominated by conscious experience—have a life of their own. For the attentive reader, this declaration translates itself into the exclamation, "This could be me!" or "This *is* me!" It is what one senses at the beginning of *The Divine Comedy:*

> Midway the journey of this life I was 'ware
>> That I had strayed into a dark forest,
>> And the right path appeared not anywhere.
> Ah, tongue cannot describe how it oppressed,
>> This wood, so harsh, dismal and wild, that fear
>> At thought of it strikes now into my breast.
> So bitter it is, death is scarce bitterer.
>> But, for the good it was my hap to find,
>> I speak of the other things that I saw there.

> I cannot well remember in my mind
> How I came thither, so was I immersed
> In sleep, when the true way I left behind.
> (tr. Laurence Binyon)

And similarly at the beginning of *The Pilgrim's Progress:*

As I walked through the wilderness of this world, I lighted on a certain place where was a Den, and I laid me down in that place to sleep: and, as I slept, I dreamed a dream. I dreamed, and behold, I saw a man clothed with rags, standing in a certain place, with his face from his own house, a book in his hand, and a great burden upon his back (Isa. lxiv. 6; Luke xiv. 33; Ps. xxxviii. 4; Hab. ii. 2; Acts xvi. 31). I looked, and saw him open the book and read therein; and, as he read, he wept, and trembled; and not being able longer to contain, he brake out with a lamentable cry, saying, "What shall I do?" (Acts ii. 37)

Dante's dark wood midway through life and Bunyan's Den in the wilderness localize the indeterminate plight of a man thrown into the dream world. The dreamer brings with him the whole burden of personal problems which the conscience has made acute. He thus stands perplexed on the threshold between two worlds, strangely aware that some significant action impends.

When the artifice does not take the specific form of a dream, emblems or threshold symbols having a similar suggestiveness may introduce the narrative and also propel the subsequent narrative action. If it is well drawn, the emblem will evoke associations, like the dream, of a sudden passage into the unknown.

In *Moby Dick* Melville half playfully offers the emblem of a swinging sign on which the words *Spouter-Inn* and *Peter Coffin* are inscribed. It greets Ishmael at the inn where he is to spend several nights before joining the *Pequod* crew in its tragic pursuit of the white whale. The emblem anticipates the two symbols of the quest: the whale itself and the coffin-turned-lifebuoy through which Ishmael is finally saved.

Early in the first chapter of *The Scarlet Letter* one comes upon the rosebush growing wild outside the prison door through which Hester Prynne will shortly emerge. The rose is the standard emblem of sexual passion and romantic love—a love that has tragic consequences. The emblem indicates a typical predicament: Hester's erotic commitment to the minister. It thus serves to prefigure the main events of the narrative. Thereafter the rosebush is superseded by the complementary emblem of the scarlet letter, representing the community's judgment of an act which Hester cannot personally accept as being more sinful than the rosebush. The scarlet letter completes the meaning of the rosebush. It is as if the emblem of the rosebush introduced a fearful indeterminacy which the emblem of the scarlet letter subsequently clarifies and gives full meaning to. The one anticipates the other like a threat or a promise, or both; and as the former is gradually fulfilled in the latter, we may trace the course of the oppositional relationship and eventual reconciliation between Hester and the community.

The community punishes Hester, publicly denying her, as it denies itself, the personal dignity and trust of self-reorientation. Her role is to merge her "sin"—the wild passion represented by the rosebush—with the social ostracism indicated by the scarlet letter. The letter worn on her bosom like a rose becomes the rose in all its tragic implications in a living instance. In interweaving the two so that they become one, Hester "atones" for the community's "sin" as though it were part of her own. In this way, too, she proves society's import in the individual and the individual's import in society. These moral qualifications give the fearful, mysterious character of the emblems a remarkable coherence as they are progressively fused in the story—a coherence which brilliantly fulfills their original dreamlike indeterminacy and suggestiveness.

The emblem outlines a concise picture in brief focus. The threshold symbol generally frames a brief preparatory action of the hero and is the thematic center of a whole episode. The watery shipwreck in *The Tempest* and the incident in the Den of Errour which initiates the action in *The Faerie Queene* are forceful examples of threshold symbols. At the beginning of *Moby Dick* a threshold symbol is immediately brought into play when Ishmael pauses to wonder at a silent throng of Sunday citizens standing hypnotized by the motion of the sea. The incident forecasts Ishmael's own journey as the exploration desired by "almost all men," who "if they but knew it . . . sometime or other, cherish the same feelings towards the ocean with me."

Many of Kafka's stories begin with a pointed episode curtly delineating the hero's plight and the moral condition to be elaborated in the rest of the work. The beginning of *The Castle* instantly concentrates the feelings of severance, isolation, and remoteness in the unapproachability of the castle; and all are symptomatic of K.'s pervading problem: finding his own identity by learning his relationship to others:

> It was late in the evening when K. arrived. The village was deep in snow. The Castle hill was hidden, veiled in mist and darkness, nor was there even a glimmer of light to show that a castle was there. On the wooden bridge leading from the main road to the village K. stood for a long time gazing into the illusory emptiness before him.
>
> (tr. W. and E. Muir)

The Trial begins as starkly, with an overarching sense of siege. It renders immediately the moral predicament of the hero in his abrupt divorce from the familiar and the routine:

> Someone must have been telling lies about Joseph K., for without having done anything wrong he was arrested one fine morning. His landlady's cook, who always brought him his breakfast at eight o'clock, failed to appear on this occasion. That had never happened before. K. waited for a little while longer, watching from his pillow . . . but then, feeling both put out and hungry, he rang the bell. At once there was a knock at the door and a man entered whom he had never seen before in the house . . . "Who are you?" asked K., half raising himself in bed.
>
> (tr. W. and E. Muir)

The same tone of baffled constraint pervades the description of Gregor Samsa waking to an unreal reality at the beginning of *The Metamorphosis*:

As Gregor Samsa awoke one morning from uneasy dreams he found himself transformed in his bed into a gigantic insect. He was lying on his hard, as it were armour-plated, back and when he lifted his head a little he could see his dome-like belly . . . What has happened to me? he thought. It was no dream.

(tr. W. and E. Muir)

Such initial characterizations introduce the hero in immediate symbolic focus at the threshold of his experience. In Kafka, however, they often seem an ironical inversion of the dream induction. Kafka's heroes wake from a dream to a world which appears more illusory—more baffling and more demanding of inner consciousness, since it is the dream of "real life"—than the sleep of the past from which they have just emerged. But the same inclusive relationship (symbol-dreamer-plight) is present in both the dream induction and its inversion.

Generally the hero (Dante, a Christian, Hester Prynne, or Ishmael) starts out in despair to face an unprecedented ordeal. The progress of this ordeal provides the whole sequence of action for the ensuing allegory. The dream of the real world is the world of the narrative—the world of unmitigated moral consciousness where every experience has a greater possible value than the hero can himself detect. The meaning he gives his experiences will be partial and indeterminate if he lacks the confirmation of others. He may have a choice of guides, who will either help or mislead him. But, if he does not accept a guide, he invariably misleads himself and is doomed to tread through the mazes of the self-insulated labyrinth his consciousness becomes. Or his choice of the wrong guide will reveal some incapacity for pursuing the "true way"; for what misleads and deters him is always a personal fault, sometimes a serious disability. Here again one recalls Dante's moral distinction between wakefulness and sleeping, as well as T. S. Eliot's recent gloss on it, "distracted from distraction by distraction."

In many allegories the dream artifice hints at the degree of consciousness the hero needs in order to cope with his situation. That Dante at the beginning of his quest cannot pass beyond even the least forbidding obstacles and must have Virgil's aid through Hell and Purgatory indicates the didactic and emulative character of the quest. The path through the unknown is partly opened up by the counsel and guidance of his fellow poet, who previously has gone most of the way. But the medieval poet's initial sense of personal sin and despair clearly invites a Christian solution beyond Virgil, or toward which Virgil, the avatar of reason, serves as a gauge.

In *The Faerie Queene* Red Cross (Holiness) first appears with the Lady Una (Truth):

> Ycladd in mightie armes and silver shielde,
> Wherein old dints of deep woundes did remaine,
> The cruell markes of many a bloody fielde;
> Yet armes till that time did he never wield.

The greater part of the subsequent allegorical action issues from the initial identification based on this association: Holiness cannot find its way without Truth, and vice versa. The particular talents required for facing an ordeal—for which, though he has not yet been tried, Holiness is nevertheless certified—are later detailed in elaborations of the original arms-and-shield metaphor. We also learn that both his extreme innocence (the preface describes him as "a tall clownish younge man") and the fact that the Queen has chosen him are vital qualifications for the success of his mission.

Like Red Cross, Bunyan's Christian at first displays little more than his singular innocence. But his innocence turns out to be as crucial as it is lucky. For though it instantly misleads him, it is part of his original certification (the Bible he carries) and an expression of his unredeemed condition (the burden on his back). It propels him from the Slough of Despond, where the Evangelist rescues him, to the House of the Interpreter, where his quest is characterized as an imitation of Christ, and onward to the Cross, where he loses his burden. Important as innocence is to begin with, it means nothing without grace or the conviction that one has been elected for salvation. We learn this later through Ignorance, a disingenuous pilgrim, who goes a considerable distance along another way but eventually fails to receive a heavenly reward.

That Kafka's heroes persistently refuse the didactic aid of helpers or choose the wrong ones is the reason why they fail; and it is why, after tireless machinations, they so often face defeat when they suddenly realize they have scarcely even begun. It is as though the typical formula for the Christian hero, which Dante set up and Bunyan renewed, had been adapted by Kafka with all the old terms intact save the consolation of a supernatural grace. Kafka's incomplete adaptations of the formula suggest those picture puzzles appearing in the old Sunday supplements under the caption, "What's Wrong with this Picture?" Thus challenged, the guileless reader would soon discover the unlikely three-legged table, the one-eyed girl, or the boy without a nose. The lack of real helpers, with the implication of some disorientation in the guiding intelligence, has a determining effect upon the allegorical narrative. This condition relates directly to the values which the writer gives to consciousness and unconsciousness.

The dream is a vigilant reminder of life in the depths of unconsciousness. Like sleep, the physical state that makes dreaming possible, it resembles the vast unregenerate condition of chaos so quickly brought under control in the first verses of Genesis. The relation between sleeping and dreaming would seem to depend as much upon a physiological necessity as upon some control by mind, an indwelling intelligence. Just as sleep is traditionally equated with the will-less chaos of mind and matter before imagination and form have been imposed on it, so the dream, in turn, suggests the stirrings of intelligence toward wakefulness and order. Out of sleep the creative spirit, the light dividing the darkness, will move, having been fed and invigorated by rest.[3] Sleep may be viewed as a regressive respite corresponding to the recurrent night-journey in myths. In *Insight and Outlook*, Arthur Koestler has described the basis of this correspondence as "a regression of the integrative tendencies, a crisis in which the mind undergoes an atavistic relapse—to return refreshed and ready for a higher form of synthesis. It is once more the process of regenerative equilibrium, of a *reculer pour mieux sauter;* the integrative drive, having lost its bearing in trivial entanglements, has to go back towards its origins to recover its vigor."[4] But myths and religious doctrine always differentiate between the beneficial and the harmful sleep—with the axiom that death, the last sleep, will entail either a punishment or a reward.[5] It is insisted that the design of some transcendent intelligence governs the journey of consciousness, both sleeping and waking. The same notion appears in allegory, where characters do not simply and innocently fall asleep, or dream meaninglessly.

Frequently, the allegorical hero is constrained from falling into an unrelieved sleep. If he does fall asleep, some aspect of his fitness to carry on is impaired. To Spenser's goal-directed knights, Guyon and Red Cross, sleep comes when they are least capable of proceeding directly to their quest. They evidently succumb to some need in themselves to give up the struggle. Either because of accumulated strain or some particular temptation, they can no longer endure the tension involved in withstanding it. Sleep not only arrests them, it often abandons them to the destructive powers of original darkness, for which the ethical equivalents are despair, pride, lust, or, as it may be, the very sins it is their special duty to overcome. Even Christian, Bunyan's indefatigable imitator of Christ and Paul, is caught napping soon after losing his burden; he is immediately—though only momentarily—deprived of his scroll, his ticket to heaven. Only the oblivion he fearfully enters at heaven's gates, the baptism of death, has permanent value: it purges his soul so that he may share the nameless comforts of the blessed. When Melville's Ishmael or others in the *Pequod's* crew fall asleep or are washed into the sea, they lose their fellow-feeling and their sense of mutual dependence. Part of original darkness, the sea is an oblivion which crazes and kills; at the end only Ishmael is saved from it. The frequent lapses of Kafka's heroes into an uneasy sleep, particularly when some major revelation is impending, signify their inability to understand their own problems.

The artifice of the dream, then, is the body of techniques sustaining the impression through the narrative that it is all dream-like. It is no casual device but a function of the allegorical procedure as a whole. In fixing the symbolic character of the quest, it discloses the hero's relationship to his goal. It keeps a realizable purpose alive by dramatizing the dominant sanctions and forces with which the hero must keep in touch. It also conveys the serious tone of the make-believe, designating the transcendent import of the matter experienced by the dreamer.[6] Typifying the procedure is a guiding, usually beneficent intelligence that impels and even shares the hero's consciousness.[7] Sometimes it is that part of divinity present in each man, or it is the corrective effects which reason and imagination can have upon the consciousness. It may be expressed through the magical governing art of an exiled duke (Prospero in *The Tempest*), or through the interpretative genius of a zealous reformer-impostor (Don Quixote or Melville's Confidence Man), or through the urgencies of memory and epiphany (as in Proust and Joyce) shaped in the declassed conscience of the esthetic hero. In this way the guiding intelligence articulates distinct cultural and religious ideals.

Since the Renaissance such an intelligence seeks to bring authority closer to actual social and psychological needs than medieval doctrine allowed. An aspiring mind with its own ethical aims accompanies a nationalistic and self-battling Puritan conscience; these attitudes impel the Protestant missions of many allegorical heroes. It becomes clear, for example, that if

Red Cross is the redeemer of Truth from the Errour of the Roman Church, he is also the Protestant hero triumphant, prefigured in Revelation, who militantly re-enacts the symbolism of that emancipation. Moreover, he is Britain's national hero, St. George, supported by Arthur's thaumaturgy and the language of Arthurian symbolism. When he redeems Truth's parents, in the figures of Adam and Eve, he takes on the aspect of a militant Christ among the money-changers, while triumphing over distinctly Elizabethan enemies at home. Even more centrally, he is also an aspect of Christ in the Harrowing of Hell. Similarly, as Christ's imitator and preacher, Bunyan's Christian walks and talks within an ambience not of kings, noblemen, and churchmen, but of provincial English journeymen and small merchants. And the Vanity Fair he traverses is at the same time a symbolic adaptation of the Book of Revelation, a Babylon seen through Protestant eyes.

The guiding intelligence in each case demonstrates a new vision of paradise regained. If, according to Spenser, England is to become an earthly paradise, it must first be a Protestant kingdom under Elizabeth. If, according to Bunyan, the way to heaven leads through England, not knights but enthusiastic and semi-literate provincials (a new heroic class) will be walking and preaching, Bible in hand, under the invisible eye of God, who looks approvingly at such "mechanics." The importance of Revelation to both allegories is that it invokes a new national, prophetic authority to speak for the ethical ideals of emergent sectarian movements.

The same critical attitude vitalizes the fiction in Swift, Melville, and Kafka, where the guiding intelligence is Protestant and self-questioning as well. For Swift the corruptions of Queen Anne's reign, which Gulliver transfers to various mythical island kingdoms, are continually being measured against ethical and psychological, but also physical, transformations in Gulliver himself. And it is finally Gulliver, as impartial observer, ingenious projector, and resourceful hero, whose last account of himself depicts a defeated man alienated from society altogether. We are asked to use our brains, our passions, and our experiences to understand the reason for his transformation, and the condemnation of society it implies. We meet something of the same challenge in Melville's Confidence Man. A paragon of Christian charity who makes fraudulence profitable in the various guises of an impostor, he seems gradually to victimize himself. Then, on the verge of resolution, he moves into the nebulous dawn of reality, trailed by the paradox that truth is indistinguishable from the illusion through which it must somehow be communicated. From such an elusive hero it is only a step to Kafka's accused men, the apparently free, respectable white-collar workers who are suddenly incriminated by the law. The law permits them to witness its inexorable restraints and corruptions while refusing to answer their most urgent questions.

In all these instances the Protestant vision of a regained paradise has been systematically dismantled by an intelligence that finds it deceptive, by an imagination that feeds on the indigestible facts of human experience. Abounding grace, national pride, even the lesser virtues of resourcefulness and charity, give way to the all-pervasive ordinances of the superego. To the hero the voice of authority amplifies his own exacerbating sense of guilt. Pursued by his conscience, he finally has the choice of renouncing the quest, of elevating mock principles into a missionary illusion, or of offering himself up as a scapegoat to impenetrable legalisms that masquerade as divine dispensations. In any case, his sense of mission seems morbid or ludicrous rather than salutary. Instead of being a pronounced vindication of his own standards, his fate turns into a misjudgment involving the loss or disfigurement of the self.

The dream artifice, or the inverted presentation of a hypothetical world resembling a dream, colors the whole allegorical fiction. In fixing character and ordeal, emblem or threshold symbol, symbolic narrative language and thematic resolution, the artifice takes on an authority of its own. The question asked by the Freudian analyst regarding the psychic origin of the dream, its latent meaning, and its symbolism (How far is the dream generic, and how far is it individual?) may be applied in allegory to the dynamics of the dream artifice. Both the dream and the dream artifice dramatize and give identity to objects and events ignored by the conscious mind. The dream, however, compounds the private experience of the dreamer with the typical experience, symbolically expressed, of all dreamers. In both the dream and the dream artifice, the search for meaning, the whole interpretative effort, starts from the personal character of the dream itself. After its personal character is understood, one proceeds to the generic expression, where performance reveals the judgment of conscience. The connection between the generic and the individual, the typical and the personal, may never be demonstrable in much detail. But in going any distance toward an answer one begins to discern the range of complex relationships which the dream involves for the artist, the analyst, and the reader, who are all dreamers.

3. *Talisman and Initiation: Signs of the Hero as Missioner*

In the dream artifice, as in dreams generally, objects and persons often are recognized immediately because of the patent incongruity of their associations with other objects or persons. The strange becomes curiously familiar because like Alice in Wonderland one instantly attaches to it one's own labels and emotional claims. This experience resembles the glimpse we are first given of the allegorical hero. Before we know *who* he is we discover *what* he is. We are asked to recognize him first by physical signs: his clothing, his burden, the paraphernalia he carries. And the sense of these, the hero's credentials, is frequently epitomized in some talismanic object belonging to him. Of this signification the hero himself may be only dimly aware; he is apparently more conscious of what he is intended for than of his own personal identity. Spenser's Holiness is prepared from the beginning for a mission of redemption. He knows the mission will include Una and a dragon-slaying. But he does not know, until he sees the New Jerusalem, that the mission will lead to his becoming a figure for St. George. Here the existential situation expands as the allegorical meanings accrue from all the hero's actions, until it seems to dominate the causal dialectic.

What makes the character a hero is not merely the social sanction that has been invested in him to begin with, but more significantly the sanction he earns through his own actions and through the integration of his consciousness. The character is potentially heroic, and, although he does not know this, his way has been marked out; he is simply not conscious enough at the start to know. What he does and how he does it will widen and deepen his consciousness, and prove his destiny. But because the element of chance is omnipresent—a real and an illusory sense of freedom, until the very end—there is always some doubt that he will succeed or that his integration will be complete. His situation at different moments may seem utterly unenlightened and even foolish until he himself comes to sense the pattern of consciousness he is attempting to create. In the opening of the Bhagavad-Gita, for example, the hero asks, "Why should I fight?" and the answer is "Keep on fighting." But whether the hero succeeds or not, the growing consciousness of a purpose controlled by increasing self-realization is what makes his story an allegory. The identification of the hero's mission through his talismans is particularly well drawn in Melville's *Confidence Man*.

The Confidence Man, an impostor-hero, emerges vigorously "at sunrise on a first of April . . . suddenly as Manco Capac at the Lake Titicaca, a man in cream-colors, at the water-side in the city of St. Louis."

His cheek was fair, his chin downy, his hair flaxen, his hat a white fur one, with a long fleecy nap. He had neither trunk, valise, carpet-bag, nor parcel. No porter followed him. He was unaccompanied by friends . . . it was plain that he was, in the extremest sense of the word, a stranger.

Following his "advent" aboard the ship *Fidele*,[8] he joins a crowd perusing a placard that offers "a reward for the capture of a mysterious impostor, supposed to have recently arrived from the East."

The Confidence Man is obviously associated with the sun: he is like Manco Capac, the Inca sun god; he arrives at the springtime and Fools' Day of the year; he is the impostor from the East; in his passage he is "evenly pursuing the path of duty, lead it through solitudes or cities." And all these associations are corroborated in the color of his complexion and clothing, and by his unassisted arrival. The moral counterpart to these disclosures is that he comes like the sun to shed light (enlightenment); and, as if to minimize the blunt report indicated on the placard, he soon holds up for the passengers' better view a black slate. On it he successively writes and erases a string of maxims from 1 Corinthians 13: "Charity thinketh no evil"; "Charity suffereth long, and is kind"; "Charity endureth all things"; "Charity believeth all things"; and "Charity never faileth." [9] He is protected from the jeering spectators by the way he bears these maxims "shield-like . . . before him," and by his humble ("gentle and jaded") and innocent ("lamb-like") appearance, and finally by the fact that he is a deaf-mute. Subsequently when he falls asleep in front of them ("he seemed to have courted oblivion") he succeeds by this ruse in disarming their suspicion, whereupon he reappears in a series of other disguises. Behind each disguise he challenges the credulity of the ship's passengers—"an Anacharsis Cloots congress of all kinds of that multiform pilgrim species, man." In the final chapter, it is still as a solar representative (the Cosmopolitan) that he enters the darkened stateroom "where burned a solar lamp, swung from the ceiling" which "the captain required to be kept burning till the natural light of day should come to relieve it." Here he ministers to his last auditor, a weary, credulous old man, whom he finally leads away in the "waning light" of the expiring lamp.

Melville compacts into the hero's solar character additional aspects of "originality" [10] by manifold analogies with each new talisman the Confidence Man flaunts. From first to last, from deaf-mute to garrulous Cosmopolitan, the sun-stranger focuses each of his avatars in a distinctive talisman. All these talismans are equated first with the multiple doctrine he sells (trust-confidence-optimism-geniality-liberality-magnanimity), then with the physical substances he offers (patent medicines, investment stock, dutiful boys to be employed instead of machines), and with the gold coin he receives in payment. The ramified effect is initiated by the deaf-mute writing on the black slate. It is intensified by the Negro cripple ("who, owing to something wrong about his legs, was, in effect, cut down to the stature of a New-foundland dog") and his tambourine, which he identifies with the sun-as-baker (warming "der stones fo' dis ole darkie when he sleep out on der pabements o' nights"). And it culminates in the opulence of the philanthropic Cosmopolitan, who sums up all previous transformations:

A cosmopolitan, a catholic man who, being such, ties himself to no narrow tailor or teacher, but federates, in heart as in costume, something of the various gallantries of men under various suns. Oh, one roams not over the gallant globe in vain. Bred by it, is a fraternal and fusing feeling. No man is a stranger. You accost anybody. Warm and confiding, you wait not for measured advances. And though, indeed, mine, in this instance have met with no very hilarious encouragement, yet the principle of a true citizen of the world is still to return good for ill. My dear fellow, tell me how I can serve you.

In this manner Melville aims at creating through his multiple hero a total effect which, as he says, "will be akin to that which in Genesis attends the beginning of things." It is a composite effect, quickened in each episode by a pertinent talismanic object that identifies and gives meaning to the hero's new disguise. There is a similar emphasis in *The Scarlet Letter*, where Hester and her letter are so closely associated that they come to be thought of as inseparable. The letter is a magical object: Hester's creativity, her love, and her punishment are all vested in it; it is her badge and triumphant shield. Unless one notices how it is first borne in public "so fantastically embroidered and illuminated on her bosom," one misses its cumulative force in the characterization and narrative which follow. The letter sustains Hester's every action; it also reflects and measures the actions of the persons directly implicated with it, as well as those who merely glance at it. When it appears as a brand on her lover's chest and as a sign in the sky, the letter seems to universalize Hester's passion into a cosmic symbol. Hester's talisman catalyzes developments of character and action without basically distorting them.

This manifold use of the letter shows how the talisman becomes an active token of the hero's consciousness. Symbolic of authority or magical purpose, and denominating the heroic mission, the talisman reflects his will and the means of his strengthening it. Like a sceptre or Aaron's rod, it condenses heroic attributes in one object. Although not strictly talismans, other objects, like articles of clothing, may possess talismanic properties if they are associated with the hero. They may serve to prefigure his mission long before any clearly individualized delineation is drawn. The hero's physical appearance is often so cogently portrayed as a declaration of what he is that this description suffices for identification without further amplifications. His typicality, observed immediately from external signs, is enough to stamp him, as it does the first appearance of an actor on the stage, with an intensely dramatic presence. In this way the personified forces in allegory carry something of the traditional authority not only of dramatis personae but also of sacred figures in myths.

For the allegorical hero, as an exponent of cultural experience, generally faces a labyrinthine pattern of action which is archetypal.[11] The wider implications of this action, understood as an achievement of complete self-consciousness, unfold in the dramatic episodes attending his ordeal. The hero first measures his capability by the obstacles he overcomes during his initiation, when approaching the threshold of adventure. These preliminary tests challenge his skill and fitness for the mission. Whether gauging moral courage or physical strength, they all indicate the degree of awareness which governs his choice. The pitfall of sleep, as we have seen, may ensnare him in a small death which he unconsciously wishes for and wearily or pleasurably succumbs to. If overcome, the obstacle will sharpen his sense of personal vigilance. If the obstacle is disabling or if only partly overcome, it will call for a renewed struggle—as does, for instance, the narcissism of John Marcher in James' *Beast in the Jungle*, which completely mocks his high-minded mission, forcing him to find his punishment in the grave of his own self-deception. In Hawthorne's *Ethan Brand* an ironical transformation of consciousness through defeat awaits the hero. Having returned home after a lifelong pursuit of the Unpardonable Sin of pride—the knowledge that separates him from other men—Brand is consumed by fire in the lime kiln, leaving nothing of himself but his hard heart that has been transformed into "special good lime." In Kafka a mistaken sense of independence and a fatal ignorance of signs along the way vitiate his heroes' quests and prove to be their undoing.

In all such instances the arrested hero fails during some initiatory act so that subsequently he never manages to embark upon the supreme test. For another type of hero, the successful passage may hinge upon a culminating and ingathering affirmation of consciousness, dramatically sustained in an ultimate act of confrontation. This occurs in James' *Jolly Corner* when Spencer Brydon encounters the specter of his other self on a middle landing of the abandoned family home. Brydon overcomes the specter he had been led to seek out and wakes to his reward in the love of Miss Staverton, his guide and helper. It also happens in Hawthorne's *Artist of the Beautiful* when after many reverses the artist, Owen Warland, succeeds in creating a mechanical butterfly which confounds his neighbors briefly before a child's hand crushes it. The implication is that the work of creation, having been accomplished against so many odds, has served its purpose in justifying the artist. Since the work has proved itself in the visible fulfillment of the artist's imagination, it no longer matters that the proof is destroyed. A similar, though much more ironic, formulation of a successful passage occurs in Hawthorne's *My Kinsman, Major Molineux,* where the young provincial hero discovers through the public humiliation of his uncle the meaning of his own quest and the freedom to make a new start.

The dramatized experience expressed in a series of actions depends upon an increasing integration of consciousness in the hero. Typical of post-medieval literature is a growing emphasis on the realistic portrayal of the hero's situation and surroundings. With this emphasis the judicial and antagonistic principles are often driven inward and only hinted at in the fictional process, rather than being externalized throughout. The talismanic power of objects and figures identifying the hero is consequently diffused or obscured; the pattern of initiation is not manifested in simple moral actions but is implicitly worked out and modulated through psychological characteristics, as shown in Kafka's *Metamorphosis.* The quest itself, except in explicitly didactic tales, becomes part of the hero's involuted responses to experience. There is a sense in all this of ramified problems leading to an unanswerable mystery, as though the appropriate key had been lost and only the scantiest clues remained.

Some explanation for the elusive pattern and the increasing ambiguity in modern allegories may be found in the destruction of the rigid base of cultural authority upon which allegory traditionally depended, and in the relatively greater stress put upon the autonomy of the artist since the Reformation. One consequence of these conditions is vividly evident in the difficulties encountered by Spenser, Bunyan, Hawthorne, Melville, and Kafka as writers of allegory.

IV

Authority

Professor Eucalyptus said, "The search
For reality is as momentous as
The search for god." It is the philosopher's search

For an interior made exterior
And the poet's search for the same exterior made
Interior: breathless things broodingly abreath

With the inhalations of original cold
And of original earliness. Yet the sense
Of cold and earliness is a daily sense,

Not the predicate of bright origin.
Creation is not renewed by images
Of lone wanderers. To re-create, to use

The cold and earliness and bright origin
Is to search. Likewise to say of the evening star,
The most ancient light in the most ancient sky,

That it is wholly an inner light, that it shines
From the sleepy bosom of the real, re-creates,
Searches a possible for its possibleness.

WALLACE STEVENS, *An Ordinary Evening in New Haven*

Since the fifteenth century the allegorical writer has been increasingly accused of practicing preachment without art, rhetoric without imagination, fantasy without reality, symbolism without mastery. To allay such criticism he has had to find ways of renewing a method that too easily lends itself to the abuse of discursiveness. This turns into the problem of finding an appropriate literary form, but more specifically of giving the allegory, in whatever form, a vital symbolic structure that is communicable in terms of contemporary actuality.

For Spenser to write a compendious epic at a time when the form had grown effete was to risk literary oblivion. As writers of "romance" novels, Hawthorne and Melville had to face a comparable problem in their time. Spenser succeeded by giving the epic form a new heroic content after the Italian pastoralists had exploited it as a vehicle for stringing fables together. Similarly, Hawthorne's and Melville's success, as we now estimate it, had a great deal to do with their directing the novel form to metaphysical purposes and away from its use as a genteel diversion.

The writer's quest for a new form probably owes much to his dissatisfaction with the dominant tastes of his time. In this regard it is tempting to compare the situation of Spenser with that of Hawthorne and Melville relative to the tastes of the two different periods.

By 1596, when *The Faerie Queene* was published in England, the new forms of national drama, interlude, pamphlet, voyage book, and chronicle history had become decidedly more popular than poetic or allegorical narratives. A new audience had grown up which fed upon themes of English legend and history, class rivalries, national contentions, and the biases for verisimilitude in the low style of comedy and farce; a psychologism of humor types and a melodramatic view of behavior extended the practice. By such standards the allegorical method in Spenser's hands would appeal mainly to courtiers, poets, and pedants, instead of the nation at large, whose ideals were precisely what Spenser was attempting to celebrate in epic form. So it appears ironical that he should have used the popular chronicle stories out of Holinshed and Geoffrey of Monmouth —the same thaumaturgical legends upon which popular taste was battening in Elizabethan adaptations on the stage—as though he might thus be doing something to overcome distaste for his method.

The parallel situation of Hawthorne and Melville in mid-nineteenth-century America was that both writers sought to create serious fiction on an allegorical basis against the full tide of the triumphant social and sentimental novel. The inveterate novel-reading public was accustomed to Scott and Dickens and to the Gothic simulacra of Charles Brockden Brown; and Fenimore Cooper's popularity was largely due to the fact that he wrote fiction with the English stereotypes of America in mind. This is the very sort of fiction Melville criticizes in *The Confidence Man:* "That fiction, where every character can, by reason of its consistency, be comprehended at a glance, either exhibits but sections of character, making them appear for wholes, or else is very untrue to reality. . . ." (Chapter 14) All his life Hawthorne yearned not so much for a Europeanized America as for a condition that would permit the kind of imaginative freedom he at times ascribed to British and Italian writers as their birthright. Meanwhile he kept writing tales based on the American past as though aware that some historical underpinning was needed to sustain his allegorical themes and characterizations. More directly, Melville employed the "foreign" setting of the sea, seeking a unique imaginative propriety in a timeless and spaceless domain against the dominant fictional practice of pasteboard characterization and historicism. Yet like Hawthorne he wove ironic legends out of the American scene and character, as though he too were trying to meet some

hidden necessity of his allegorizing fiction for a literal or historically significant dimension.

Yet the literary question for the allegorist often goes deeper
than one of coping with the tastes of his period or of seeking a
new form. The challenge of critics is only part of the greater
challenge he meets in undertaking subjects that may have had
a philosophical but only a very limited literary formulation previously. The fictional creation cannot be one thing and the
allegory, the symbolization of a philosophical view, another—as
it is in the hands of the moralizer. Fiction and allegory must be
simultaneous, a single creation. Both together must assert an
integrated vision of reality; and this creative authority must
be sustained within the work, not by any appeal to a body of
doctrine outside of it.

Considered most broadly, allegory is made by many different
kinds of writers using all the literary forms. These writers, often
widely separated from one another in time, bring literary
method and particular cultural ideals together in a flexible organization of techniques. In this way unsuspected possibilities
for literary treatment are discovered, leading to the gradual
construction of a new form or the revitalization of older forms.
The writer's need to re-create forms seems to coincide with attempts in other fields to renew cultural ideals during the same
period. And by his expression through new forms he often
comes upon a system of symbolic organization which will carry
its own creative authority in terms of those ideals. We see such
activity in the re-emergence of the pastoral poem and the novel,
and the verse and prose satire, in the seventeenth century, the
picaresque tale in approximately the same period, and the rise
of the short story in the nineteenth century. In periods of dis-
rupted and changing forms, the allegorical method struggles to
incorporate irrational material, but is subsequently curbed into
the new and increasingly stabilized forms which must contain it
until they too can be broken out of later. Perhaps this is why it
seems impossible, for example, to deal with *The Divine Comedy*
or *The Faerie Queene* simply as narrative poems or romance

epics, or with *Pantagruel, Don Quixote, Moby Dick* and *Ulysses* simply as novels. These fabulous instances tell us that the allegorical writer seeks not just a new form or a new poetic, but a new or recoverable authority for the creative imagination, an authority that often embodies all past formulations.

Edmund Spenser thought himself Chaucer's successor, but he also wished to be known as the English Virgil and Ariosto—a poet who expressed Britain's heritage as a rising nation, and whose work, full of the classical tradition, spoke to all Europe. Spenser assimilated what he found useful in the Italian romances, Chaucer, and the Latin poets: a variety of poetic techniques and ways of telling a story.[1] But when, in deference to the Renaissance custom which demanded learned apologies and critical acknowledgments, Spenser wrote a preface to *The Faerie Queene*, he revealed his uneasy situation. It is written as a letter to his friend Sir Walter Raleigh, expounding "his whole intention in the course of this work."

The preface is a curious statement. It mixes a defense of the allegorical method with an outline of a scheme based on the twelve Aristotelian virtues, by which the twelve projected books of the poem are to be understood.[2] Few of the "intentions" are fulfilled in the six completed books, although most readers have taken his remarks to be the literary key to the poem. None of Spenser's six moral virtues is purely Aristotelian in its exemplification; they all speak at least as emphatically in the language of the Arthurian myths and Christian symbolism. And far from being "a continued Allegory," as Spenser declares, the poem sustains a complex allegorical design through the first two books, becomes a personification fable in a fragmentary seventh book, and slackens into a series of isolated tales in the intervening four. The letter begins:

Sir, knowing how doubtfully all Allegories may be construed, and this booke of mine, which I have entitled the Faery Queene, being a continued Allegory, or darke conceit, I haue thought good, as well for avoyding gealous opinions and misconstructions . . . to discover unto you the general intention and meaning, which in the whole course thereof I have fashioned, without expressing of any particular purposes, or by accidents, therein occasioned.

What follows explains almost nothing of the allegorical meaning of the work as a "darke conceit," though it does fit labels to the leading figures of the various books. Moreover, Spenser seems deliberately to avoid the elucidation of "any particular purposes . . . therein occasioned." Instead he rationalizes the whole work with a courtly generalization of his time—the fashioning of a gentleman. He does, however, appeal to the epic authority of Homer, Virgil, Ariosto, and Tasso, who have "coloured" their doctrine "with an historicall fiction." And he insists, following Dante's example, on the distinction between the method of a poet and that of an historian:

For the Methode of a Poet historical is not such, as of an Historiographer. For an Historiographer discourseth of affayres orderly as they were donne, accounting as well the times as the actions; but a Poet thrusteth into the middest, even where it most concerneth him, and there recoursing to the thinges forepaste, and divining of all thinges to come, maketh a pleasing Analysis of all.

Although the distinction goes back to Plato and Aristotle, Spenser's insistence on it gives the notation more than an air of literary propriety. Restatement of the difference is called for especially in periods when the authority of poetic imagination is confounded with the procedures of social critics, moralists, historians, and theologians; and it was on this distinction that Spenser based the authority for his allegorical practice in the poem. For it is not simply the poet's alteration of the temporal scheme that distinguishes his method from the historian's. It is that in doing so he exploits what is most important to him, the imaginative center of the action. He thereby transforms history and action, and frees them from the bondage of time. He creates a new order and a new time—a permanent present where "thinges forepaste" confront "all thinges to come" without vio-

lating credibility. Perhaps it was the poetic proof of this distinction that Milton had in mind when he praised Spenser for being
"a better teacher than Scotus or Aquinas."

While mingling many literary streams of the English Reformation, *The Faerie Queene* conveys a new conception of the allegorical method. This is not to blink at the characteristic defects—at least for a modern reader: the heavy emphasis on
political and ecclesiastic squabbles, the profuse imagery exhibiting virtuosity for its own sake, and the numerous episodes of
personified morality crowding the narrative. But the poem's total richness is surely an effect of something more permanently
impressive: the fabulous amalgamations of national, classical,
and Biblical lore out of which the allegory grows. Foremost
among all impressions is the vital constructive energy which
could make out of a Renaissance worthy's stock of learning and
partisan passions, a testament of Christian ideals rooted in the
real struggles of the individual consciousness.

In renewing the epic Spenser could rely on a tradition of romance, a way of storytelling in prose and verse, without having
to quarrel seriously with the form. If others had debased it,
Chaucer, Ariosto, and Tasso had refined it; and there were the
examples of Homer, Virgil, and Ovid to show along what lines
it might be fulfilled anew. In using Platonic love as a figure for
beauty and truth, Spenser could apostrophize all other virtues
in its name and choose the means by which his own temperament would forge them into an allegorical poem. In adapting
Aristotle's active virtues, he could further centralize love in marriage and friendship so that they became dynamic symbols su-
perseding the more warlike character of the classical epics. But
in his treatment of love—and to a lesser degree temperance and
holiness as well—Spenser was celebrating not a philosophical
notion but a way of life patterned on an ethical ideal. The virtue
was active also because it permitted characters to be determined and distinguished by its means; moreover, it had the effect of showing what keeps men together in society. The virtues
thus helped to give Spenser's narrative esthetic and moral di-

mensions that do not gainsay a conviction of Christian ideality.

In fact, esthetic and moral views in the poem go together, as in Spenser's belief, for example, that the work of artifice is inferior to the work of nature. In the Bower of Bliss a sense of inherent contamination grows out of the poet's depiction of the Bower as a static artifice superimposed upon a scene of natural beauty. None of the usual mythological graces have sanctified this outlawed pleasure haven. Neither Venus nor Cupid, nor any wholesome figure of conventional romance, appears here. Elsewhere in the poem, in the House of Malecasta, in the House of Busyrane, and in the creation of the false Florimel, the symbol of an over-effusive art represents original nature contaminated by some malign hand. This seems to be saying that art destroys natural beauty by imitating or embellishing or abstracting from it as often as art reveals beauty by creating a new object in its guise. It is of course an extremely ambiguous point. For if one applied it indiscriminately to all art, even *The Faerie Queene* would seem questionable. But as applied to the work of the allegorist, by whose prerogatives the world may be transformed and presented as one gigantic Bower of Bliss, the idea elicits unforeseen consequences.

At the head of Spenser's scheme stands Nature, whose creations surpass those of the human maker. The artist's re-creation of natural beauty, his mythmaking, essentially is an act of devotion, a glorification of all created matter.[3] On these grounds the fiction may be a good or bad imitation; what it imitates is an original conceptual scheme which the allegorist strives to make over in the form of art, for pleasure and edification. The allegorist's world is essentially opposed to that of the simple fabulist's, whose moralism reduces the real world's multiplicities to a few abstractions. The romance epic Spenser created in *The Faerie Queene* indicates how an allegorical imagination, adapting the resources of past culture and the cultural ideal reborn in its own day, could organize a vision of reality which is justified through what man actually knows about himself and the world he lives in. It is a poem that justifies not the ways of God to man but the ways of man to man. In this sense, in the sense that it is a free use and fusion of all resources of knowledge within the imagination, *The Faerie Queene* deserves to be called a humanistic poem.

In contrast with Spenser's, Bunyan's apology for using allegory in *The Pilgrim's Progress* shows more doctrinal zeal than literary caution. Yet at certain points it echoes Spenser's defensive assertion in the attempt to justify the comprehensive aim of the fiction. Bunyan first notes how, his head crammed with Biblical texts and commentaries, he "Fell suddenly into allegory." He describes the sense of personal satisfaction the writing afforded—not "to please my neighbour," but "my own self to gratify." And he wishes to point out that he wrote mostly by way of happy intuition:

> For, having now my method by the end,
> Still as I pulled, it came; and so I penned
> It down; until it came at last to be
> For length and breadth, the bigness which you see.

More pertinently, he notes that allegorical design supposes alertness in the reader: the meanings "must be groped for, and be tickled too,/Or they will not be catch'd, whate'er you do." Summoning up the general authority of the Gospels for his figurative method, and the practice of worthy polemicists for his dialogue form, he continues, "I find that men (high as trees) will write/Dialogue wise; yet no man doth them slight/For writing so." His invitation to the reader is finally an appeal to accept the fancifulness of the allegory as an imaginative sport:

> Wouldst thou be pleasant, yet be far from folly?
> Wouldst thou read riddles, and their explanation?
> Or else be drowned in thy contemplation?
> Dost thou love picking meat? Or wouldst thou see
> A man i' the cloud, and hear him speak to thee?
> Wouldst thou be in a dream, and yet not sleep?
> Or wouldst thou in a moment laugh and weep?

> Wouldst thou lose thyself and catch no harm,
> And find thyself again without a charm?
> And yet know whether thou art blest or not,
> By reading the same lines? Oh, then come hither,
> And lay my book, thy head, and heart together.

Through the workmanlike bounce of the verses something of the preacher's blandishments in cajoling his parishioners is imparted. But at the same time Bunyan's questions touch directly on the psychological content of everyday wishes, common daydreams and nightmares, and thereby prepare the reader for the serious make-believe in the allegory which follows. He suggests, for instance, the possibility of dreaming significantly without sleeping, of finding the import in the "pleasant" riddle, of seeing one thing in the guise of another ("man i' the cloud"), of realizing the tragicomic essence ("in a moment laugh and weep"), and of experiencing vicariously the perplexing adventure ("lose thyself and catch no harm").

To assume that Bunyan was merely sugar-coating a prolonged sermon is to miss the considerable dexterity, frequently the extraordinary intensity, with which he tells the tale of Christian's journey to heaven. It is also to miss the quite original use of traditional and novel materials that go into its telling. In being directly addressed, the reader is asked to witness an essentially personal experience. The narrative has every appearance of an autobiographical confession, like St. Augustine's, with a setting and characters drawn from contemporary actuality. Moreover, the tale is obviously a religious dramatization of the individual soul's struggle for salvation in this life, which serves as a figure for the life to come.

Christian's quest combines elements from the stock medieval tale of the soul's pilgrimage with elements from chivalric romance depicting the embattled hero puzzling his way through to a personal reward in Christian ideality. Christian is a type of everyman finding his own sanctions without benefit of ecclesiastic dispensation; but he is also, like St. Paul, a preacher and prophet whose qualifications are all the more impressive because he has perseveringly earned them. Anyone can try to get to heaven, and indeed many almost do, but it is by virtue of his scroll that Christian succeeds, since it authorizes him how to behave and how to regard, even if quite narrowly, the behavior of others.

Some of Bunyan's portrayals of seventeenth-century types are in line with the contemporary mode of Character writing; his imagery and personification resemble the emblem, an earlier fashion of depicting what Sidney called "a speaking picture" and Quarles, "a silent parable." But Bunyan's enthusiastic gift for thinking metaphorically makes use of a pictorial device which gives his allegory a further dimension. In his, as in Spenser's case, it is likely that the pictorial art of the emblem books served as models for metaphoric illustration just as the current movies have served Faulkner and Sartre, and as Greek house- and vase-paintings may have served Virgil.

Literally, *The Pilgrim's Progress* depicts the soul's pilgrimage from the doom of life without grace to salvation. Allegorically, it portrays an everyman hero following the Christian pattern of suffering and rebirth as an initiation into heavenly life; morally or psychologically, it provides a therapy for burdened consciences. Scriptural quotations in the text give explicit analogues to the fictional action—especially as it relates to Christian's role as a proselytizer, whose duties are defined in his actions and dialectical discourses, and are meant as prescriptions for practical behavior. Parallel actions from the Book of Revelation (e.g., the flight from the doomed city, the vision of the world's end, the figure of Apollyon representing worldly law and the English Church, and the climactic vision of the New Jerusalem) are worked into the narrative. They show the social ideals of a Christian utopia, with all the revolutionary implications of establishing Christ's kingdom on earth, later amplified in Bunyan's *Holy War*. *The Pilgrim's Progress* is still fresh because the allegory fulfills a religious ideal imaginatively—that is, renews it in the rebirth of consciousness, so that the fiction finally eludes absorption or parody in any dogma.

Hawthorne's prefaces seem more objective than either Spenser's or Bunyan's; actually they are more personal and recognize an essential difficulty that accompanies his reformulation of the allegorical method inherited from Bunyan and Spenser. In his prefaces Hawthorne seldom fails to acknowledge a sense of dissatisfaction with a way of writing he could not perfect, and this tells us much about his aims as an allegorist. He was admonishing critics and readers who disapproved of his method, but he was also admonishing himself for faults he could not manage to overcome.

In the preface to *The Blithedale Romance* Hawthorne insists on calling his fiction "romance," claiming a European prerogative denied the American "romancer." Of the freedom this privilege allows the European writer he says:

. . . his work is not put exactly side by side with nature, and he is allowed a license with regard to every-day probability, in view of the improved effects which he is bound to produce thereby. Among ourselves, on the contrary, there is as yet no such Faery Land, so like the real world, that, in a suitable remoteness, one cannot well tell the difference, but with an atmosphere of strange enchantment, beheld through which the inhabitants have a propriety of their own. This atmosphere is what the American romancer needs. In its absence, the beings of imagination are compelled to show themselves in the same category as actually living mortals; a necessity that generally renders the paint and pasteboard of their composition but too painfully discernible.

The statement shows his acute perception of the shortcomings in imitative realism. Hawthorne's "atmosphere" assumes a certain literary tradition and a receptive audience capable of understanding it. The wish for a "license" to create "such [a] Faery Land so like the real world," and yet different, since it turns on its own axis, tells us what tone he hoped his allegories might have. Instead of the botch-work of a labored realism, Hawthorne proposes the autonomy of the work of art that has "an atmosphere of strange enchantment, beheld through which the inhabitants have a propriety of their own." Such an atmosphere actually permeates *The Scarlet Letter*, perhaps because in that subject he had found a striking correlative to his historical and critical preoccupations with Puritan morality. Out of a "sensuous sympathy of dust for dust," he traced his ancestors' search for freedom of conscience in a locale where the historical and moral conditions were unmistakable. In most of his fiction the ambivalence in feeling, combining estrangement from and attachment to those conditions, is portrayed by analogies with the Fall of man. Yet perhaps only *The Scarlet Letter* sustains a fictional authority that goes beyond the specific time and situation it deals with.

The whimsical, half-disparaging note in the self-portrait prefacing *Rappaccini's Daughter* carries further the complaints about his inherited impasse as an American writer. But it also pleads for a broader acknowledgment of his more successful allegories:

His [M. de l'Aubépine's—i.e., Hawthorne's] writings, to do them justice, are not altogether destitute of fancy and originality; they might have won him greater reputation but for an inveterate love of allegory, which is apt to invest his plots and characters with the aspect of scenery and people in the clouds, and to steal away the human warmth out of his conceptions. His fictions are sometimes historical, sometimes of the present day, and sometimes, so far as can be discovered, have little or no reference either to time or space. In any case, he generally contents himself with a very slight embroidery of outward manners,—the faintest possible counterfeit of real life,—and endeavors to create an interest by some less obvious peculiarity.

Here Hawthorne clearly phrases his problem with allegory: that of making the conception warmly human so that the conception can glow its way through the story. Perhaps his "less obvious peculiarity"—the distaste for which he was continually trying to overcome in the reader—is the peculiarity of his allegorical method, worked out with such tender subtlety in *Rappaccini's Daughter*.[4]

Melville's problem, like Hawthorne's, was to find a method

whereby a vigorous moral and esthetic authority could be re-created in fiction. For him, as for his predecessors, the challenge was to map out the relation of the unknown country of allegory to the known countries and conditions of contemporary actual-ity. Even Spenser, whose sense of freedom in this regard was presumably greater than Hawthorne's or Melville's, exhaus-tively summarizes the deeds of British kings from Arthur to Elizabeth and also provides a fictional history of his fairyland. Spenser's documentation gives readers some sort of foothold in fact; it reinforces his own make-believe with the prestige of tra-ditional example, and is also a concession to national pride in its Elizabethan context. Yet it seems to be a covert labor of histor-ical self-defense—one which may have been fresh in Spenser's mind when he wrote the proem to Book Two.[5] There he answers some actual or anticipated charge against the poem's being merely "th' abondance of ydle braine . . . and painted for-gery," by comparing its mystery with the latest discoveries "of th' Indian Peru," "the Amazon huge river," and "fruitfullest Virginia." Melville, in his turn, best resolved his problem in *Moby Dick*, where the allegory grows out of a sea voyage that leaves behind the social and religious hypocrisies of landlocked Christians. In that novel he made unprecedented use of factual material, creating thereby a new sort of literal dimension for his allegorical narrative. In place of the traditional materials of ro-mance, which depend upon common knowledge, Melville incor-porated within *Moby Dick* a natural history of whaling. The task called for an adaptive originality greater than the kind Hawthorne was put to in *The Scarlet Letter*. How well Melville managed it is evident when we recognize that no aspect of the subject he treats is objectively questionable. Ahab's story con-tains as inclusive a summary of whales and whaling as can be found in any text on the subject. Anything comparable may be imagined only by supposing that in order to write his history plays, for example, Shakespeare had had to invent the chroni-cles on which they are built. It is not simply Spenser's way of facing the question of authority—which meant giving substance to his work by having his figures, each with various roles, participate in both his fairyland and in the real world. Nor is it Bunyan's way, which is to build on the common reader's assumption that Christian's progress has been authorized and prescribed in particular Biblical books. Melville makes entirely explicit the very body of knowledge from which his allegory must draw its effects. He works the facts into the course of his narrative, not simply by making them depend upon historical, descriptive, or dogmatic authority, but by substantiating them inclusively in the multiform analogies they serve in his fiction.

In Kafka this deliberate construction upon objective facts becomes the substance of the fiction, though the growing insinuation of the unpredictableness of "human law" soon covers the face of the structure like a fungus. Kafka's subject is the bureaucracy of institutions and the absurd legalism of banks, law courts, penal colonies, hotels, and semi-feudal middle-European villages. By a twist of perception the happenings within a gigantic legalistic hierarchy are made to support his allegory just as the undistorted facts about whaling support Melville's allegory. In his pursuit of particulars and the compendious annotations given to the most deviant possibilities of applying the law to the event, Kafka is apparently as exhaustively solicitous of the truth of his facts as Melville is of his. Kafka's so-called realism is surely the pervading effect of his skillful focusing on every involution of the relationship between one individual and the rest of society. In sustaining the literal dimension of his narrative, his realism takes on the hard convincing texture of authenticated fact. Both Melville and Kafka seem thus to affirm Dante's method and the statement concerning it in the *Convivio*. The letter (the literal sense) is not separable from the allegory. The one contains the other, as the outside of a thing contains the inside, as the whole contains its parts—as the facts of whaling contain "the overwhelming idea of the whale," or as the applications of the law contain the law.

Only a shadow line of difference separates Melville's or Kafka's creation of a new literal dimension and the historical or mythotypical approach of, say, a Thomas Mann. In overplaying an historical source or Biblical legend, Mann places his burden of proof on an authority other than that of his fiction, so that his narrative turns into an elaborate apologia for the legend's historical or doctrinal truth. Most historical novelists ingenuously vulgarize the same procedure by relying wholly upon the documentation of a safely fixed version of authority, unlike the custom of imaginative poets cited by Dante and Spenser. Avoiding the arduous possibilities of creating a personal vision, they substitute the requisite minutiae of historical or mythological verisimilitude, and thereby produce inspired guidebooks or erotic manuals instead of original allegories.

The connection between the re-creation of authority and the allegorical method becomes more intelligible when we consider two distinctions traditionally made in ethics and esthetics. The first concerns the difference between the modes of prophecy and apocalyptic; the second, the difference between the modes of history and poetry.

In *Apocalypse* (1932) D. H. Lawrence remarks that the Book of Revelation is probably a more primitive product of the allegorical temperament than the apologists could successfully normalize—as, for example, they had normalized the dark spirit in Job or Isaiah. As Lawrence shows, the color and beast symbolism in Revelation comes out of a tradition older than any discoverable in Biblical literature. Like the symbolism in many traditional non-Christian books, it has the flavor of the old pre-rationalized myths going back to an era before the monotheistic world had been codified in Genesis. Lawrence's suggestion recalls the fundamental ancient difference between prophetic and apocalyptic attitudes. The distinction is summarized in Hasting's *Dictionary of the Bible:*

Prophecy and apocalyptic both claim to be a communication through the Divine Spirit of the character and purposes of God and his Kingdom. Prophecy believes that God's goodness will be justified in this world; apocalyptic almost wholly despairs of the present and its main interests are supramundane. Hence its adoption of pseudonymous authorship.

The same distinction is ironically expounded in *The Confidence Man* as a conflict between the openhanded prescriptions in Corinthians—represented by the deceptive optimism and worldly trustfulness of the Confidence Man himself—and the injunctions of distrust in Sirach: [6]

"Ah!" cried the old man, brightening up, "now I know. Look," turning the leaves forward and back, till all the Old Testament lay flat on one side, and all the New Testament flat on the other, while in his fingers he supported vertically the portion between, "look, sir, all this to the right is certain truth, and all this to the left is certain truth, but all I hold in my hand is apocrypha."

"Apocrypha?"

"Yes; and there's the word in black and white," pointing to it. "And what says the word? It says as much as 'not warranted'; . . . So if your disturbances be raised from aught in this apocrypha," again taking up the pages, "in that case, think no more of it, for it's apocrypha."

"What's this about the Apocalypse?" here, a third time, came from the berth.

"He's seeing visions now, ain't he?" said the cosmopolitan, once more looking in the direction of the interruption. "But, sir," resuming, "I cannot tell you how thankful I am for your reminding me about apocrypha here. For the moment, its being such escaped me. Fact is, when all is bound up together, it's something confusing. The uncanonical part should be bound distinct. And, now that I think of it, how well did those learned doctors who rejected for us this whole book of Sirach. I never read anything so calculated to destroy man's confidence in man. This Son of Sirach even says—I saw it but just now: 'Take heed of thy friends,' not, observe, thy seeming friends, thy hypocritical friends, thy false friends, but thy *friends,* thy real friends—that is to say, not the truest friend in the world is to be trusted. Can Rochefoucauld equal that? I should not wonder if his view of human nature, like Machiavelli's, was taken from this Son of Sirach! And to call it wisdom—the Wisdom of the Son of Sirach! Wisdom, indeed! What an ugly thing wisdom must be! Give me the folly that dimples the cheek, says I, rather than the wisdom that curdles the blood. But no, no; it ain't wisdom, it's apocrypha, as you say, sir. For how can that be trustworthy that teaches distrust?" (Chapter 45)

As the prototype of all shrewdly rationalizing optimists, the Confidence Man succeeds in casting out doubt by casting out the significance of the Apocryphal books.[7]

Prophecy, taking its authority from the Word of God, calls attention to the covenant, the social contract, the moral obligations of men under divine law. It rehearses the law and stresses punishable infringements of the law. Although the message of the prophets may run counter to that of the priests of an established order, the prophets, whether accepted or outlawed, are there to remind men that they have strayed from their higher social and religious duties. Apocalyptic, on the other hand, derives from the dedicated experience, isolated vision, and judgment of the solitary man, the seer, the unlicensed and obscure sage. In denying the possibility of mankind's improvement, apocalyptic casts a cold eye on man's social and moral nature, and criticizes the failures and imperfections of man and his laws. Apocalyptic frequently becomes the refuge of heretical imagination defying the contingencies of legalism and the status quo. Apocalyptic appears as the habit of mind out of which the richest allegorical paradoxes have come—the transfiguration by Dante of the courtly ideal of love, Arthurian symbolism interlaid with Revelation symbolism in *The Faerie Queene*, and in Melville the counterposing of Ishmael's "democratic" worship of the savage's idol with Ahab's arrogant pursuit of solitary vengeance.

In allegory, prophetic and apocalyptic elements often go together. In Dante's *Commedia*, for instance, one cannot easily separate the prescriptive figurations of the Gospel or the vehement condemnations of political abuses from the visionary revelation of the mystic Rose. When it is directly concerned with reinforcing the truth of a traditional text or myth, the emphasis is prophetic. When it concerns the personal vision supported by preliterary lore, apocryphal books, the anonymous symbolism of the dream, or, more significantly, the knowledge derived from the contradictory nature of experience, the emphasis is apocalyptic.

It is not surprising, therefore, that apocalyptic expression should so often be condemned and banned as obscurantist, or overblown and normalized by sanctimonious interpretation, as the Book of Revelation has been—since it feeds many hopes and many vanities. In fiction expressing a dominantly apocalyptic element, as in Melville and Kafka, the search for authority turns into a real pursuit through the still wild and unconquered parts of consciousness. Where the prophetic element is dominant, as in Bunyan, the search seems strenuous rather than strange, even a bit predetermined, like proceeding down a well-lit path in a jungle behind a friendly savage. In the uneasy merging of prophecy with apocalyptic one senses the influence of a Platonic bias, which achieves an ideal transformation of the world by consigning the actual world to perdition and then consoling it with the blueprints of a thoroughly methodized utopia. Perhaps in this sort of reluctant intransigency lies buried the old vision of paradise regained, which Platonists recurrently seek to salvage from what, to them, the actual world must always represent: the ruins of paradise lost.

On another level, the connection between the re-creation of authority and the allegorical method may be considered in the light of the old controversy over the divergent claims of history and poetry. For history, as an authentic record of events and persons in the past, becomes authoritative in lending itself to interpretative and moralizing purposes, as in Plutarch, Gibbon, Spengler, or Toynbee. As soon as the past is recorded and interpreted, it takes on a re-created, almost legendary, form in our consciousness of reality. Insofar as the poet, broadly the creator of fictions, treats the same historical subjects, he is said to be "imitating" reality in a double sense: as the whole known history of the human consciousness, and as the unique core within every happening, which is scanted by the historian. To the degree that the poet renders some aspect of the past which has already been documented by the historian, he does not improve the historical record, but must always be thought of as distorting (abridging or adding to) it. One assumes that what justifies his activity is some beneficent effect of his mimetic powers: by changing the historical emphasis he surprises and entertains an audience and illuminates forgotten but pertinent truths.

The poet's role, in this regard, will remain completely subservient to the historian's unless it can be shown that he creates something quite different from a version of history—something which, in fact, has nothing to do with either ascertaining or reaffirming the "truth" of history, but which is true-in-itself. According to Aristotle, the poet creates not a version of reality but a vision of what is probable: he hypothesizes by imitating the action of life; and when he does this well his work becomes "an organism" having a self-contained structure. Subsequently, in the literary critic's extension of this opinion, the poet is credited with a propriety similar to that of the philosopher of science: he is thought to bridge other modes of inquiry by his use of metaphorical hypotheses and ideals common to them all. But this opinion seldom relates the structural autonomy of the poet's work to the metaphorical means by which he achieves it. The question of how this is done is intimately engaged with the question of authority, which we have examined in the works of several allegorists.

The process of re-creating authority through the intensity of a free-flowing action tempers fictional method and ideals into pliable toughness; thus the re-creation of authority cannot be considered apart from the developmental process of the literary work. In this sense the allegorist's work has little or nothing to do with the practice of philosophers, historians, or theologians, except as their particular structures suggest a similar hypothetical treatment of reality. For the allegorist the re-creation of authority necessitates a critical view of reality, a re-examination of the objective norms of experience in the light of human ideality. It includes the making of a new version of reality by means of an ideal which the reality of the fiction proves. In Dante's "state of souls after death," Spenser's fairyland, and Bunyan's "similitude of a dream," we see how different versions of historical reality are provided for in terms of a dominant ideal. The dominant ideal in each instance succeeds in making the fictional reality transcendent so that contemporary issues of belief thus located, as it were, in high relief cannot be better grasped in essence than from the works themselves. Generally in historical novels, the exclusive dependence on textual authority supersedes the possibility of autonomy in the work. The work tends to become an historical commentary, an interpretation of the history which has everywhere within the book been made to support it. In such fiction we do indeed get a bastard product: at best, a version of history which if not factually questionable must forever remain esthetically questionable.

We may now look at the typical figurative means by which allegory reaches autonomy through its fictional method.

V

Identification

"I am myself a great lover of these processes of division and generalization; they help me to speak and to think. And if I find any man who is able to see a 'One and Many' in nature, him I follow, and 'walk in his footsteps as if he were a god.' And those who have this art, I have hitherto been in the habit of calling dialecticians; but God knows whether the name is right or not."

PLATO, *Phaedrus*

"But is analogy argument? You are a punster."

"Punster, respected sir?" with a look of being aggrieved.

"Yes, you pun with ideas as another man may with words."

"Oh well, sir, whoever talks in that strain, whoever has no confidence in human reason, in vain to reason with him. Still, respected sir," altering his air, "permit me to hint that, had not the force of analogy moved you somewhat, you would hardly have offered to contemn it."

HERMAN MELVILLE, *The Confidence Man*

AN ALLEGORY starts from the writer's need to create a specific world of fictional reality. Like the divine creator in Genesis, he ordains the reality by designating it according to function: "Let there be light: and there was light. And God saw the light, that it was good. And God divided the light from the darkness." His reality comes into existence and comes to mean something at the same time. Each allegory starts with a *tabula rasa* assumption, as though the world in its view were being made for the first time. The double purpose of *making* a reality and making it *mean* something is peculiar to allegory and its directive language. In this it differs from the univocal aim of realistic fiction, which imitates the world-as-is from a view reduced to the commonplace and assumes only what may readily be taken for granted throughout. In fixing and relating fictional identities, allegory gives new dimension to things of everyday acceptance, thereby converting the commonplace into purposeful forms.

The symbol in allegory means something both literally and as a trope—that is, as a thing and as the quality of that thing, analogically conceived—before it is understood as being used and developed with other kinds of trope in an extended fiction. The medieval symbol of God's hand, for example, signifies power, yet the symbol is not thought to be merely equivalent with the abstract quality we call power. It is taken quite literally as God's hand *and* as a sign for power in the sense that God's creation *and* God's operative law are manifest together in all natural events. The symbol expresses both an event and a cosmic outlook based on a belief in divine purpose as set forth in the Bible. In *Moby Dick,* "the overwhelming idea of the whale" is the allegorical unit that points to the comprehensive fictional-historical development of the theme in the novel. As the exposition of whaling proceeds there is a gradual evolvement of correspondences with the whole of life.

Like the development of a musical theme, the amplified statement based on the trope becomes the mark of the work's allegoricalness: the whole work partakes of it and also fulfills it. The allegorical unit then resounds with innumerable connotations. The tension between the theme and its inherent meanings is built up on all levels of connotation so that the reader is drawn into the extended allegory until the expository data appear to be serving, say, Melville's purpose in a way parallel to the way Christian analogy served for the medieval writer. To put this somewhat differently, the fictional scheme governing the hypothetical aspects of the literal sense and giving the allegory its lifelikeness must seem to be determining the story's figurative meanings all along the way. It must seem that the meanings grow naturally out of each action in the narrative. The more complex a writer's grasp of psychophysical relationships, the richer the work is likely to be. For the meanings of allegory depend, as in poetry, upon the accretion of certain tropes. These tropes make evident a consonance between objective facts and their moral or psychological counterparts, so that the reality— the hypothetical nature of the literal—is ultimately transcended by the total organization of meanings which is the fiction itself. And so one may say that the language of allegory makes relationships significant by extending the original identities of which they are composed with as many clusters of meaning as the traffic of the dominant idea will bear. In this way allegory as an extended trope may include the functions of all other tropes—metaphor, irony, metonymy, and synecdoche.

To discern the relevance for allegory of such relationships entails noting how things are identified and developed in typical narratives. The assumption here is that analogy, irony, and dialectic transfer are distinctive verbal modes in allegory. These modes should accommodate any view of the working processes in allegory without requiring much unusual terminology and the irksome consequence of constant definition.

1. *The Expanding Analogy*

The simplest and most widely serviceable form of analogy is
the allusion, which tends to underscore the moral character of
objects and ideas. Its effectiveness lies in its immediacy and ap-
propriateness, which in turn assume the reader's recognition of
its source in some archetypal story or situation. The Old Testament and the Gospels are the bases of allusion in medieval allegory; Greek and Roman mythology—more particularly, Virgil
and Ovid—in Renaissance allegory. Later allegorists have
drawn upon these and additional sources, in an ever-widening
range of allusion, from history, science, and comparative mythology. Bunyan's Biblical tags and marginal notations represent the most explicit sort of allegorical allusion. Another
variety, frequently exploited by Hawthorne, occurs in this description of Hester Prynne:

Had there been a Papist among the crowd of Puritans, he might
have seen in this beautiful woman, so picturesque in her attire and
mien, and with the infant at her bosom, an object to remind him of
the image of Divine Maternity.

Such an allusion works epigraphically. It sums up the myth or
doctrine from which the correspondence is drawn, and focuses
it briefly but memorably. In this way the allusion confirms what
the reader may already suspect is true of the character's situation. And by indicating the writer's bias, it also stresses the usefulness of that supposition, in all its implications, throughout
the fiction.

When allusion is used to introduce a specifically purposeful
action—as in the figure of Prince Arthur in *The Faerie Queene*,
who, among his other roles, has the one of divine grace, and
hence always acts providentially—it may recur like a leitmotiv
in many parts of the narrative. Embodied in a central figure
like Bunyan's Christian, it may even encompass the whole work;
then, because the figure continually recalls the Gospel stories,

the work itself becomes one great allusion to those stories. When the allusion is used in an alteration of the traditional account of the myth from which it derives—as in Lawrence's *Man Who Died*—it reconverts the dogma into a new mystery. Thus the kind of allusion a writer adopts discloses the tonal or ideational quality of his indebtedness to some tradition of thought or belief; and the way he uses the allusion also discloses the degree of his dependence on that tradition and something of his total aim.

Personification in its many varieties is another form of literary analogy. When most explicit it becomes a sledge hammer in the hands of the writer, making resoundingly evident what cannot possibly be mistaken. Christian's swift progress from the City of Destruction to the New Jerusalem is prefigured in the active virtue Christian personifies. One cannot then complain that Christian's pace through sloughs, byways, and mountains seems so marvelously unimpeded. If the point of the personification is forgotten, the reader may unwittingly be charmed by sulky Ignorance, who prefers his own company when he is outtalked by Christian. Thus beguiled, the reader will later deplore the trick, which, "even from the gates of Heaven," tumbles Ignorance into Hell for lacking the proper credentials. Such a reader has evidently neglected Bunyan's warning to "Put by the curtains, look within my veil," and must seek his own fate with Ignorance himself. Otherwise the personified virtue or defect is likely to disappear in the character's perverse attractiveness.

The personification works more inclusively when, instead of being run along in parallel units for instructive comparison, opposing figures are actually related and sustained ambivalently throughout the narrative by alternately interchanging attractive and repulsive characteristics. The conflict and tension rising from such ambivalence is usually highly dramatic. This is the effect of the alternating guises of Duessa (Duplicity) and Archimago (the black magician representing Fraud and Hypocrisy) upon the monotypic figures of Una (Truth) and Red Cross (Holiness) in *The Faerie Queene*, whereby the fabulous

and contradictory nature of experience is explored more exten-
sively than the doctrinal lesson. Una and Red Cross are both
affected psychologically as individuals striving to fulfill themselves in the virtues they represent, and also, more broadly, in
the actions they undertake—actions which typify certain aspirations (national, mythical, political, and religious) of immediate contemporary significance. But they are dramatic characters
too: always something more than the virtues they personify, being helped to their humanity by their susceptibility to the vices
or states of mind which the Duessas and Archimagos beguilingly personify. Consequently the sense of ambivalence in the
personification is often as arresting in Spenser's narrative as the
dramatic device of twins and mistaken identity in Shake-
spearean comedy. But in addition, at the base of Spenser's
personification resides the doctrinal exemplification; a religious
psychology always takes this foundation for granted in any individual experience.

With more complex views of experience, such as we get in
Hawthorne, Melville, and Kafka, the ambivalent personification, though framed in a religious dualism whose doctrinal base
has crumbled, seems to measure the distance that exists between the world of appearance, chance, and self-deception,
and the world of reality, order, and truth. With them the contradictory nature of experience springs from just this sense of
what the distance signifies: a self-embattled condition which
develops when the rupture between "worlds" is recognized in
every human action. This ambivalence runs through the passages on the whiteness and proportions of Moby Dick. Against
the mystery and invulnerability of his antagonist Ahab's pride
is magnified, now into a personal heroism, and now into a monstrous monomania. In the fundamentalism of the Confidence
Man—a swindler representing all the social virtues and disguised as a Christian idealist—we see the ambivalence mount
until it finally prevents us from fully accepting or fully rejecting
him. A similar tension develops in Kafka's rationalizing hero.
His defeat seems somehow predetermined by, and yet fatally

disruptive of, some need for order in a world which so unequivocally judges him.

In implementing thematic ambivalence, personifications of this sort are intensified by the further resources of analogy. These may be described as functioning in five important ways: analogy through nomenclature; correspondence of a state of nature with a state of mind; implicit comparison of an action with an extrafictional event; manifestation in an action of a state of mind; the allegorical waver.

First and most patently, the analogy through nomenclature is allied to the personification of abstractions: the use of an attributive name that, as it constantly designates an event, person, idea, or quality existing outside the story, builds up a sense of like identity in the fiction. Didactic narratives commonly identify some trait by the name of the agent who dramatizes it, especially the type character. Linguists have surmised that the custom of designating things by attributive names is the first evidence of metaphor in language. The device—actually a metonymy—is familiar in Aristophanes, the moralities, Elizabethan and Restoration drama, and in most romantic and satiric novels. It pervades popular literature of all sorts: ballad, popular song, comic strip, pulp story. Modern writers as sophisticated as Mann and Joyce are especially partial to the device. Henry James' notebooks show his engrossment with questions of character and place names, and in practice James leaves little doubt that he intends such names to carry an extrafictional force of reference. It is clear that each writer who prizes the particularity of his characters hopes, by the names he gives them, to suggest both their uniqueness and their universality, if not the thematic role they fulfill in the action. In Melville the symbolism inherent in the name Ishmael, for example, works at every turn much as the whole group of disguises of the Confidence Man does.

Secondly, there is the analogy which compares a state of nature with a state of mind. The underlying anthropomorphism is a commonplace in Romantic poetry and in all pantheistic creeds.

The aim is to bring realistic instances together in a single ideal, e.g., the Many in the One, and thus raise the hope of human transcendence over environmental limitations. Physical nature is praised in order to confirm the immanent role of human consciousness reflected there. The benignly human appears to inform all insentient things. If a rock can feel pain or a tree be made to bleed, then sermons are manifest in flowers and stones, passions engraved on clouds. In the very act of numbering the natural elements, of dividing the year into seasons, the seasons into months and weeks and days, one makes nature a storehouse for all sorts of archetypes, fates, and salvations. The whole idea of personifying the mute or inanimate in nature is of course a way of humanizing it—that is, feeling tender toward it by uniting with and gaining control over it. The personification, then, is as much a matter of reading benignity or malignity into, as of reading it from, the evidence of nature.

In the Red Cross–Una vs. Archimago–Duessa formula, Spenser's personification gives human attributes to the concepts of virtue and vice. The concepts have grown from the experience of many instances and from generalizing upon experience and reapplying the virtue and vice in other situations. One might say that in Spenser the analogy works from mind to nature, while in romantic anthropomorphism it works from nature to mind and thereby introduces another factor: a generalization upon human attributes which is confirmed by being recognized in nature.

Another analogical resource is the elucidation of states of mind by appropriate actions. A fine multiple instance extends throughout the first book of *The Faerie Queene*. It is worth reviewing in some detail since it illustrates the type more substantially than would any number of briefer examples.

When Red Cross succumbs to sleep in Archimago's hermitage, or to the giant Orgoglio while embracing the false Duessa, or to the arguments of the old man Despair, the experience may be understood as essentially psychological. But at the same time each experience is another phase of the ordeal that tests

Holiness for the final act, the redemptive slaying of the dragon besieging the castle of Una's parents. In each situation the power of self-delusion is (temporarily at least) significantly stronger in the Knight than any talisman with which he is armed. We begin to observe that to be noble is not only difficult but also extremely enervating. It is therefore important, in noting this, that directly before each defeat Red Cross has been engaged in an action which he does not clearly consummate. Since Red Cross is unrelieved by repentance when he slays Errour (equivalent on one level to Henry VIII's destruction of the monasteries), the action initiates a string of consequences which only breed further errors and new deceptions. The action immediately results in the separation of Red Cross from Una, his true mistress. It also opens the way for the unholy triumvirate—Sansjoy, Sansfoy, and Sansloy—to do their worst to Holiness and Truth. Thus when Red Cross kills Sansfoy, he inherits Duessa, who leads him to the House of Pride where he momentarily overcomes Sansjoy. But Sansjoy is rescued by Duessa and, with the help of Night, is secretly conveyed to Hell, where his wounds are healed.

Meanwhile, although accompanied by a lion (suggestive of British national policy), Una is compelled to stay with the females Ignorance and Blind Devotion until the black magician Archimago, disguised as Red Cross, rescues her from a lesser evil only to introduce her to a greater one. By now the vengeful Sansloy meets Archimago and, mistaking him for the Knight, overcomes the magician, kills Una's lion, and makes off with Una. For his ineffectual murder of Sansfoy earlier, Red Cross is presented with Duessa, who is responsible for Sansjoy's resurrection and for Sansloy's kidnapping of Una. Although Red Cross finally escapes from the House of Pride, the exertion, partly wasted upon the unfinished business, has obviously sapped his strength; thus weakened, he is easily captured by Orgoglio. At this point only Arthur can save him and reunite him with Una. Arthur arrives providentially to break the chain of illusion with a power that transcends the black magic of the Knight's enemies.

> No magicke arts hereof had any might
> Nor bloody wordes of bold Enchaunters call,
> But all that was not such as seemd in sight
> Before that shield did fade, and suddeine fall . . .

Radiating the light of daytime reality, Arthur kills Red Cross's captor, Orgoglio, the illusion of Pride, who is now clearly exposed for the first time:

> But, soone as breath out of his brest did pas,
> That huge great body, which the Gyaunt bore,
> Was vanisht quite; and of that monstrous mas
> Was nothing left, but like an emptie blader was.

He also routs Duessa and gives Red Cross a baptismal charm; in exchange, Arthur is given, appropriately, a copy of the Gospels.

Still unrepentant, Red Cross is immediately confronted by Despair—a likely aspect of the unkillable Sansjoy. Here only Una's fortuitous aid saves him and herself for the ministrations of the House of Holiness, that spiritual hospital where the Knight learns the difference between lust and fruitfulness, where the spectacle of the seven deadly sins in the House of Pride is obliterated by the counter-vision of the virtues, and where his role of St. George, the national redeemer, is verified by a glimpse of the New Jerusalem. Arrayed as a double champion—anointed by the pagan Arthur and invested with the national holy orders—the Knight is now prepared for his three-day fight and victory over Satan, "the old Dragon." Then, in restoring the land (original paradise) to Una's father (an avatar of Adam, "most mighty king of Eden fayre"), he restores the ancient kingdom of Britain to its rightful historical eminence in the world.

From this summary of the main events in Book One several things may be concluded about the effects of analogy in Spenser's allegory. On one level the interdependence of Red Cross and Una is sustained in accordance with the doctrinal formula which they personify: neither Holiness nor Truth may triumph, or even proceed, without the aid of the other. On this level the doctrine is filled out by many distinctly local or contemporary allusions. For example: Spenser's Holiness is also an English knight, a national champion like St. George, certified for his mission (to bring the new Protestant faith to Britain) by a virgin Queen (Elizabeth), and by the sanction of a partly legendary Prince Arthur. Similarly Una, both when in distress and when acting as Red Cross's guide, is a virgin representing a romantic ideal, a Christian ideal (through her besieged parents, the parents of mankind), and a contemporary (Elizabethan) ideal.

Duessa and Archimago are also amplified as antagonistic principles by local and contemporary allusions. On this level, of course, the relational terms of analogy have little to do with elucidating states of mind by appropriate actions. They serve rather as a commentary on certain political and historical situations in Spenser's England. On another level, however, where the narrative actions seem to illustrate states of mind in the hero we come upon a universal dimension of the effects of analogy in the allegory. Spenser may not have been aware of his narrative's implications on the level we call states of mind. Yet for the modern reader the story, like other literature of the past, can be appreciated by way of its psychological implications, quite aside from the issues of the time in which it originated. It is not that such implications were not already latent in Spenser's view of sin, which derives from a tradition of moral realism as old as Virgil and Augustine. Rather, in addition to what is latent, the modern reader brings something of his own recognition of "states of mind," focused by the psychological discoveries of his own age. By following the main narrative lines in Spenser one can pinpoint the psychological aspects of the allegory. The analogical relationship in terms of local allusions and the relationship in terms of states of mind are complementary, so that one finds oneself reading *into* as well as *from* the literal story meanings that often raise the issues of the past into a continuing present.

Another kind of analogy is the correspondence of an action with an extrafictional event which the action enlarges upon. This type is similar to the epigraphical allusion in immediately concentrating attention on the analogue. It differs of course in that it is more substantially suggestive and ranges more widely through the fiction. In *The Scarlet Letter*, for example, Hawthorne first describes the scaffold "as a portion of a penal machine" on which Hester Prynne is made to reveal her shame in public display "to the surrounding multitude, at about the height of a man's shoulders above the street." The scaffold reappears later when Dimmesdale stands upon it alone in the dead of night:

And thus, while standing on the scaffold, in this vain show of expiation, Mr. Dimmesdale was overcome with a great horror of mind, as if the universe were gazing at the scarlet token on his breast, right over his heart. On that spot, in very truth, there was, and there had long been, the gnawing and poisonous tooth of bodily pain.

The third time we see the scaffold, when Dimmesdale mounts it to confess to the crowd, it suggests not simply the historical penal machine ("which now, for two or three generations past, has been merely historical and traditionary among us"), but, more strongly, the Cross on Calvary. In the glow of this implicit identification with the Crucifixion, Dimmesdale, supported by Hester Prynne, bares his stigma to the assembled parishioners:

With a convulsive motion, he tore away the ministerial band from before his breast. It was revealed! But it were irreverent to describe that revelation. For an instant, the gaze of the horror-stricken multitude was concentrated on the ghastly miracle; while the minister stood, with a flush of triumph on his face, as one who, in the crisis of acutest pain, had won a victory. Then, down he sank upon the scaffold! Hester partly raised him, and supported his head against her bosom.

By a similar correspondence Kafka identifies the hero of *A Hunger Artist* with Christ on the Cross when, after completing a forty-day fast, the artist is supported out of his cage by two specially chosen women and his impresario.

The impresario came forward, without a word—for the band made speech impossible—lifted his arms in the air above the artist, as if inviting Heaven to look down upon its creature here in the straw, this suffering martyr, which indeed he was, although in quite another sense; grasped him round the emaciated waist with exaggerated caution, so that the frail condition he was in might be appreciated; and committed him to the care of the blenching ladies, not without secretly giving him a shaking so that his legs and body tottered and swayed. The artist now submitted completely; his head lolled on his breast as if it had landed there by chance; his body was hollowed out; his legs in a spasm of self-preservation clung close to each other at the knees, yet scraped on the ground; and the whole weight of his body, a featherweight after all, relapsed onto one of the ladies, who, looking around for help and panting a little —this post of honor was not at all what she had expected it to be— first stretched her neck as far as she could to keep her face at least free from contact with the artist, then finding this impossible, and her more fortunate companion not coming to her aid, but merely holding extended on her trembling hand the little bunch of knuckle-bones that was the artist's, to the great delight of the spectators burst into tears.

The effect is notably different from Hawthorne's. Kafka's minute report, ostensibly so dispassionate, achieves a moral impact because it is so intently *seen,* a virtue lacking in the Hawthorne passage. The Artist's severe dedication, his belief in his own inviolability, is rendered through an ironic spectatorship which scrutinizes the least detail of the public exhibition. The sense of a greater meaning rises from the extreme realism of the scene. The symbolic becomes viable through an honest and effective confrontation with the reality of appearances, as in an equal battle with an honored antagonist whose measure is fully taken. Hawthorne is more concerned with registering and editorializing upon the vague public response to a symbol which remains, for the reader, undisclosable in reality. That the report of Dimmesdale's self-revelation is in effect a weaker irony is partly confirmed later when the parishioners, like some readers, fail to believe what they were supposed to have seen. But the basis of analogy is the same in both cases. Like Dimmesdale, the Hunger Artist sins out of pride in his calling, behind which he hides his human inadequacy. For this he asks forgiveness at the end, explaining that he had to fast because he could not help it, and "because I couldn't find the food I liked. If I had found it, believe me, I should have made no fuss and stuffed myself like you or anyone else."

Neither allegorist intends the analogy to be taken as a literal reconstruction of the episode described in the Gospels. Hawthorne and Kafka adapt the episode in order to fortify carefully developed symbols of their own: Hawthorne, the scarlet letter and the scaffold, which are harmonized allegorically; Kafka, the cage where the Artist undergoes his fast, and the carnival at which he is ironically exhibited as a martyr. The analogy on the scriptural episode fuses these symbols with a powerful cultural image which the reader cannot help recognizing. The analogy presents a re-enactment of Christ's ordeal, but it is not aimed at supplying a doctrinal example, as with Spenser or Dante. Hawthorne and Kafka seem to be saying that in the situations they set forth the Crucifixion can only be shown obliquely, as an irony. The irony becomes terrifying and credible because it is revealed as an actuality of daily life which repeats the original archetypal situation of Christ's lonely death on the Cross. Passing into fiction in this way, the scriptural event is given a new and different, one might say more starkly religious, value from the one now rigidified in the dogma.

There is, lastly, the use of analogy which places most of the weight of a narrative's meaning on correspondences evolved within the story itself, depending hardly at all on borrowings familiar to the reader. When unsuccessful, the attempt often lapses into a kind of analogical baiting or teasing of the reader. When successful, the analogical elements are continually balanced in what may be called an allegorical waver—an illusion that is gradually discerned in much the same way that faces are glimpsed and finally focused on in a picture puzzle showing a profusion of foliage.

Analogical baiting and the allegorical waver are associated with the more familiar conventions of coincidence and foreshadowing. The telescoping of time (i.e., coincidence) and the weaving of seemingly intrusive details into the narrative (i.e., foreshadowing) are the oldest, perhaps the most primitive, conventions of storytelling. They occur in all fables and myths, and especially in allegory. Although a patent artifice is often annoying, coincidence and foreshadowing are used by skillful writers in such ways that even a perceptive reader is willingly beguiled. In symbolic narratives they increase in value the more other fictional means—e.g., verisimilitude and simple chronology—are dispensed with. These conventions can seldom be managed, however, without considerable skill. The handling of them is a delicate matter, involving the imaginative balance of the whole work. If the coincidence and foreshadowing are overinsistent the symbolic intention quickly becomes too obvious. On the other hand, where verisimilitude and chronology are heavily emphasized, the symbolic intention may disappear. In either case the dominant emphasis soon reaches a point of diminishing returns.

A good allegorist tends to strip his narrative of the accidentals, partly to achieve greater symbolic intensity, partly to make evident the identification of the event or character with its function in the story. But, if the device is revealed, the identification will seem arbitrary and the fiction will cease to convince. Hawthorne, for example, often obscures the very substance of moral credibility he is trying to create through coincidence and foreshadowing, by continually surrounding them with mountains of historical and verisimilar details. In *The Marble Faun* Donatello's faunish ears and Hilda's dove- and pigeon-like attributes become ludicrous in a laboriously created environment where these attributes lose their plausibility because of the incongruent insistence that they be taken as symbolic. But similar devices in *My Kinsman, Major Molineux*, and in *Rappaccini's*

Daughter, far from seeming ludicrous, are what make for a dramatic tension between symbol and event, and bring the action to an intriguing climax. Such disparities in effects often crop up in Melville's shorter fictions. The point is not only that the devices are easily mismanaged but that there is something basically determining about their use.

Possibly the matter will be made clear if we distinguish between the analogy that simply dangles before the reader like an artificial bait and the analogy that fully engages him in a lively interplay between fact and fantasy. In making this distinction we refer again to the term analogical baiting to indicate the former situation and to the allegorical waver to indicate the latter.

Why should the analogy between Donatello's ears and those of the marble faun, introduced in order to symbolize the youth's amoral nature, appear labored in its effects throughout the novel? The answer may be that Hawthorne's use of the analogy does not permit the possibility of extension; it does not budge beyond itself, but remains fixed at the threshold of the story. That it is intended to be the novel's central metaphor, to which the author alludes time and again, seems only to add to the burden of comparison it struggles with. It does not move the reader except painfully.

Similarly in Hawthorne's tale *Egotism; or, the Bosom Serpent,* the analogy between a morally reprehensible trait and an actual serpent consuming the heart offers a crude fantasy in the guise of a physical fact. The physiological implication, which one must try to imagine, is that something like a tapeworm is consuming the egotistical heart. Yet a tapeworm is properly at home only in the intestines; even if the parasite managed to enter the bloodstream it would have to turn into something quite formidable in order to swallow the heart. Neither the image nor the proposed fact is acceptable; the analogy stresses only the incongruity. The moral defect Hawthorne tries to elucidate has been so heavily baited with a distorted physical fact that even a gullible reader is unwilling to be taken in. Analogical baiting is as objectionable as the crudest form of personification. One is instantly struck by the arbitrary nature of the correspondence. The crude analogy, like the crude personification, does not lend itself to transformation, whereby it becomes credible and active on several levels of meaning. Instead, unable to move on any level, it negates the allegorical function it was created for—to make the fiction imaginatively self-sufficient.

A successful attempt in coordinating the several levels is achieved in the allegorical waver when they seem to proceed simultaneously and without incongruity. There are two instances of this in *Young Goodman Brown*. One evolves from the name of the hero's wife, Faith. The name is common enough ordinarily, and especially in the Puritan community where the story takes place. But in supporting the story as a moral quest, the name becomes a constant center of identification; around it flow all the implications of the hero's dependence on, separation from, and eventual rediscovery of his wife. The figure of the wife has the force of a central personification; in her the narrative events come together as a total experience that is unsuspected until the end of the tale. Similarly, the detail of the stick that looks like a serpent—that "might be seen to twist and wriggle itself"—may be taken on the factual level for "an ocular deception, assisted by the uncertain light." On another level it is vitally relevant to Brown's search for and subsequent disillusionment with the faith of his ancestors, which is the real theme of the story. These correspondences in the story are interwoven with the gradually evoked meanings of Faith: mainly truth, as continually crossed and contaminated by deception. The name concentrates in itself all that has developed, and fully comes alive as the one lesson experience has to offer when Goodman Brown exclaims, "With heaven above and Faith below, I will yet stand firm against the devil!"

In Kafka's *Metamorphosis* the principal analogy, between the self-abandoned salesman and the giant insect, also has the power of a concentrative accumulation. The analogy combines aspects of the hero's physical, social, and psychic plight with all the connotations of rejection, worthlessness, contemptibleness, and the final voiding of the insect body. Throughout the story the analogy effects a wavering between the appearance and the reality: Is Samsa really an insect? Is Samsa really human? He (or it) is both.

The allegorical waver is an oscillating movement continually held in balance between two levels of correspondence—one realistic, the other symbolic. In reading the story one sees them come together—just as one sees two points of light which flick on and off quickly in a certain fixed time relation gradually coalesce into one apparently uninterrupted band of light. In contrast to analogical baiting, the allegorical waver serves to stabilize the allegory as a self-contained mystery. With all its meanings impacted in the narrative, the propriety of the story is such that by no extrinsic reference to logic, history, or dogma can one reach outside the story to reassure oneself as to what has taken place and what has been evoked inside of it. Rather, the matter of what the story means is one that exists solely between the reader and the story; the reader takes it as he will or can, making of it what is possible to him.

2. *Irony: The Meaning of Incongruity*

Irony is felt immediately through the rapid conversions and the startling juxtapositions of dissimilars. Like all analogy, irony accumulates and condenses meanings with the force of poetic imagery. It first proposes a basic congruence between two things which have a patent incongruence underlying them. Then it presents for consideration certain instances of this incongruence, but uses these to reinforce the proposed view of congruence, as though the obvious and basic dissimilarity could not really matter. In effect, then, the absurd possibility of similarity, or even of equivalent and interchangeable identities, is momentarily taken as a serious fact. Irony pretends in this way to confirm a union of opposites by giving abstractions a context in experience that points up the problem of their conjunction. Hence irony is the traditional mode of the satirist hunting down the disparities which are understood to exist between man's moral and physical natures, between all sanguine expressions of hope in social ideals and in benevolent intentions and the unregenerate condition of human actuality. In satire irony is the chief instrument of the writer's critical aims; and these are continually being brought to the surface in a figure of speech or an inversion of terms that emphasizes by deliberate distortion. Where satire becomes an extended fiction irony takes up a much larger job that is related to the comprehensive uses of allegory.

From *Gulliver's Travels* to the tales of James and Kafka, a central character in the guise of narrator is the instrument of the author's ironical purpose—preparing, slanting, prefiguring, and finally pulling the action together. This character is generally an ingenuous innocent, a fair-minded observer, a critical and passionate lover of truth. But as it turns out, it is precisely his extreme reasonableness that victimizes him and reveals the extent of his self-delusion. That is, instead of presenting the problem straightforwardly, the author takes an opposite tack, beguiles the reader into agreement, and then by extending the substance for agreement to its absurdity, shocks by showing what the argument is really made of.

The author's agent is thus a figure palpably not the author himself who renders the dimensions of a world that is morally transformed by a disturbingly absurd but unarguable vision. One recalls Swift's philanthropic mass murderer in *A Modest Proposal*, his scheming projectors and scientific naturalists, and his curiously ingenious linguist-surgeon-mechanic voyager, Captain Gulliver. The agent appears as Melville's punctilious and conscience-stricken businessman in *Bartleby the Scrivener*, and as the self-effacing scholar-gypsy mariner, Ishmael. He is Kafka's historian in *The Great Wall of China*, the pathetic animal heroes in *The Investigations of a Dog* and *The Burrow*. He is also the double protagonist whose oppositions collapse in a culminating action: Don Quixote-Sancho Panza, the two William Wilsons, Jekyll-Hyde. In fixing the point of view in a central character who reflects the author's beliefs through their reverse image, irony makes possible both the tone of the story as a moral exploration and the nature of its resolution as an extended trope.

Irony constantly stresses the startling impact of appearance on reality as the conjunction which forms the existential situation in the fiction. Thus moral and metaphysical concerns are always inseparable from the context of some physical circumstance or action, or of a whole framework of connected details. So the staggering naturalistic documentation of the whale in *Moby Dick* supports at every turn Ahab's struggle with the phantom of evil he is hunting down in the whale and in himself. And so Gulliver investigates and minutely reports upon the newly found lands of pigmies and giants, where he lets himself be treated first as a huge beast of burden, then as a pet weasel. Subsequently his deluded compliance "cuts him down to size" in a utopia whose citizens are horses gifted with reason and where he himself is only a slightly exceptional Yahoo. He is finally gripped by the same sense of alienation that overwhelms those disillusioned victims of a nightmare passage, Hawthorne's Ethan Brand and Goodman Brown, and Kafka's Joseph K.

One effect of Swift's twofold use of irony throughout the fiction is that the worlds of appearance in Lilliput and Brobdingnag have a reality partly evolving from, but also partly independent of, Gulliver's view of them. This effect owes something to the fact that Swift attempts to depict the social and political conventions of early eighteenth-century European society. In this light Gulliver's compliance and pathetic pride reflect shortcomings in the bland optimism and humanitarianism of the contemporary European. But the reality of Lilliput or Brobdingnag always exists aside from Gulliver's view because the reader recognizes in these kingdoms much of his own contemporary world of actuality. By contrast, the reality of Houyhn-hnm-land and of the scientific wonderlands of Book III is ostensibly more factitious. It reflects not the historical world so much as the projected utopias of nationalistic aspirations which make Gulliver a culture hero. These worlds seem to be wrought out of Gulliver's and his countrymen's complacent optimism, and, more specifically, out of a greater delusion than Lilliput or Brobdingnag, so that Gulliver's suffering is greater, as if in punishment for the pride he takes in his own era's cultural projections.

In *Moby Dick*, again, the world of charted and uncharted seas which Melville documents is the domain of the whale in all its known and mystifying manifestations. The reality of this world may be gauged apart from Ahab's search and self-consuming vision—even, to some extent, apart from Ishmael's more dispassionate, exploratory view—as the world of objective knowledge taken from the context of early nineteenth-century whaling. But it is Ahab's monomania, his luckless pride and recriminative aspirations which convert the white whale, and with it the whole natural world, into an antagonistic phantom of evil. The reality of the world of appearance there presented has its own validity in the fiction; but this reality is also conditioned by the moral-ironical view of appearance, given through the eyes of Ishmael, Melville's *raisonneur*, which transforms it.

As a support for the writer's larger purpose, irony is often employed in episodes of exemplification. Pageantry or pageant-like exhibitions in allegories are staple instances of this use of irony. On the surface the incidents and processions that occur in Spenser's numerous gardens, dens, temples, and courts offer a number of diverting interludes, if not a surfeit of moral personifications. Although halting the main action they usually tell us something about the hero's psychological state. One indication of this has already been mentioned concerning Spenser's Red Cross. By witnessing or participating in such pageants, the Knight is directly affected in his will and consciousness. Forming vital links in the action leading to the fulfilled mission, the pageant may strengthen or change the course of that action; or it may simply echo, as a dramatic chorus does, the effects of specific actions. Such instances occur in the opening and the culminating sections of *The Scarlet Letter,* in the final episode of *My Kinsman, Major Molineux,* and in the linking "gam" chapters of *Moby Dick.* They are used significantly in Bunyan's chapters on Vanity Fair, and in the stories which Kafka's heroes evoke from others who by their own accounts illustrate the operations of law court or castle. The pageant shares the broader function of dramatic irony: the reader or spectator learns of a new development before the hero experiences it.

The "descriptive" and "digressive" elements noted in Dante's characterization of his method (in the letter to Can Grande) suggest the way the pageant works as an allegorical inset within a larger narrative action. Such an inset occurs in the first book of *The Faerie Queene.* While dallying with Duessa in a grove, Red Cross plucks a bough for a garland, and the bough begins to bleed. It then tells the ominous story of Fradubio—"once a man . . . now a tree." Fradubio owes his unhappy situation to the same Duessa with whom the Knight happens to be disporting at the moment. A similar episode—concerning the "bloody babe" Ruddymane—marks out the mission of Sir Guyon, the Temperance Knight, at the beginning of Book Two. There is an allegorical inset concerning Sir Trevisan flying from Despair; another in Book Two, in the tale of the jealous husband Malbecco and the adulterous Hellenore; and another in the Squire of Dames tale in Book Four. An inset device in *The Castle* introduces the story of the outcast Barnabas family, which illustrates a situation paralleling that of the hero, who, crucially enough, happens to be listening to the story. In *Moby Dick* each ship the *Pequod* meets on its journey toward the white whale offers an alternate interpretation of the whale and Ahab's obsession with it, and the episodes dealing with each constitute allegorical insets. Each disguise of the Confidence Man hints at a previous role he has played and foreshadows a new one he will shortly undertake. In a similarly comprehensive way Gulliver's voyages may be understood as four self-reflecting aspects of one character, whose fortunes add up to a multiple enactment of the theme of pride. In the course of Gide's *Counterfeiters* the inset device can be found telescoped into an inscribed figure on a coat of arms which is so constructed that the same figure repeats itself infinitely on its own ground.[1]

Finally, for the unfolding of the basic thematic ambiguity, irony provides an apparently endless continuum of integrative allusions. In this way it engages the allegorical action as a whole. This development is unusually well illustrated in one of Hawthorne's most remarkable allegories, *Rappaccini's Daughter*.

The central action takes place in a nineteenth-century Paduan garden—a setting which Hawthorne immediately heightens at the start by alluding to the Genesis account of the Fall and the Vertumnus myth. This allusion is enhanced by references to Dante and by the story's romantic emphasis on a frustrated and self-deluding love. Beatrice, the heroine, is inevitably identified with Dante's Beatrice. But she also is linked to a classical Pomona and a Biblical Eve. The convergence of these allusions at various points of the narrative allows the reader several choices in relating the total action with any of the initial referents. Dante's story of Beatrice, culminating in the *Commedia*, ends happily as the hero recognizes her redemptive role in the figure of divine grace. In the classical legend, Vertumnus, after several hazardous attempts, manages to enter Pomona's garden, and finally succeeds in winning her as his bride. Interestingly enough for the story, its meaning as a spring fertility legend, where Vertumnus represents the new season, and Pomona, the fruit-bearing trees, gives further scope to Hawthorne's implications. In Genesis, Adam, the garden's first inhabitant, eats the fruit of the Tree of Knowledge; relative to this act Eve, like the Devil, becomes an instrument of divine agency. Hawthorne's Beatrice, like Pomona, seems unattainable in her garden, although Giovanni, like Vertumnus, finally manages to enter by subterfuge. Like Eve's, her destiny is fateful; but like Dante's Beatrice she is innocent and, if rightly estimated by the hero, possesses the power of illimitable grace.

Since these allusions are implicit in all relationships between the characters, they cannot be thought disjunctive or peripheral to the story. Hawthorne's irony works them into the narrative actions so that his characters are always being measured or reflected by them. Beatrice's father is Dr. Rappaccini, the ingenious experimental scientist who, in his zeal, mixes worthy aspirations with inhuman means for accomplishing them. Baglioni, the "good scientist," envies and yet regards him as an unspeakably sinister man. But Baglioni's intentions are themselves far from being unalloyed. This is repeatedly indicated in the story, particularly when he sums up Rappaccini: "Wonderful man indeed; a vile empiric, however, in his practice, and therefore not to be tolerated by those who respect the good old rules of the medical profession."

Rappaccini's masterwork is his garden—"the Eden of the present world," where the gardener himself, "with such a perception of harm in what his own hands caused to grow," is identified with its Adam. If Rappaccini is like Adam, Beatrice is like Eve in that her body was produced out of his, and, like Eve with the tree of good and evil, she is associated with the poisonous shrub which Rappaccini created and which she calls sister: "At the hour when I first drew breath this plant sprang from the soil, the offspring of his science, of his intellect, while I was but his earthly child." The toxic effect of this association between the girl and the plant is to make of her an untouchable beauty—actually an inhuman ideal, an unwitting temptress, a *femme fatale.*

Rappaccini's intention—the result of superior intellect and knowledge—is perversely godlike, and therefore appears related to original sin. It is to endow Beatrice as a woman "with marvelous gifts," to make her invulnerable to life's harms and evils: "to be able to quell the mightiest with a breath," to be "terrible" as she is "beautiful," rather than a "weak woman, exposed to all evil and capable of none." Rappaccini also tries to make Giovanni invulnerable so that he too "stands apart from common men," and so to send them both, in superhuman magnificence, a new Adam and Eve, "through the world, most dear to one another and dreadful to all besides."

But Rappaccini's purpose is deflected by the white magical power of Baglioni, the humanitarian scientist, who indirectly causes Beatrice's death. The implication is that it is the anti-toxin he belatedly offers—motivated by envy of her father's genius—that, in disturbing the effect of Rappaccini's drugs, actually kills her. Moreover, Giovanni, whose love and faith might have rescued her, is also responsible for her death when his love reveals itself as lust, and when his distrust of her and of himself—evident in Beatrice's last words to him: "Oh, was there not, from the first, more poison in thy nature than in mine?"—causes her fatalistically to take the antitoxin he gives her.

Beatrice, like Eve, is contaminative from the start, though, unlike Eve, she is a carrier of evil rather than evil in herself. As a woman who can be transformed through love, she may redeem herself and her lover if he will fully accept her. Because he fails her she dies, the victim of his recriminative fear. Although the story ends when Baglioni bawls out to Rappaccini, "And is *this* the upshot of your experiment!"—not a question but an invidious exclamation uttered "in a tone of triumph mixed with horror"—at the end Hawthorne leaves the moral problem open.

One may now measure the force of analogy between the outcome of this story and that of each of the legends. Vertumnus did rescue Pomona, Dante did gain entrance into Paradise through a recognition of Beatrice's role as divine grace, but Adam was indeed "lost" by following Eve. Hawthorne's resolution partakes of all three allusions, but the ambivalent irony, climaxed by the intermediacy of Baglioni, adds something which is lacking in the other stories: the interdependence of good and evil, the tempter and the tempted, and the interchangeable functions of God and the Devil. In this involvement, the story offers a striking parallelism with the theme of *The Scarlet Letter*, that is, the futile attempt to isolate evil in a world where good and evil are inseparable becomes itself the greatest of evils.

Baglioni's is the voice of self-righteous piety and orthodoxy. He destroys the garden of love (the perverted ideal of love in the illusion created by Rappaccini's magical ingenuity), relying on a do-good zeal which is fired by his hidden envy of Rappaccini's superiority. Hawthorne's irony converts Baglioni's illusory benevolence into an actual malevolence as great as the malevolence he attempts to overcome in Rappaccini. Baglioni kills not only Beatrice but also the one redemptive power capable of turning evil into good: he kills love.

Similarly, Rappaccini's self-righteous unorthodoxy becomes a version of the sin of pride, mixing an inhuman scientific ideal with a fanatic's monomania, which succeeds in perverting the nature of love. Finally, Giovanni's narcissism, which can see in Beatrice only the fearful image of his distrust of love, accedes to her destruction while thinking to help her, and so becomes an instrument of Baglioni's campaign against Rappaccini. Thus Hawthorne's open resolution, including and then advancing beyond the themes of all three antecedent legends, becomes an ironic commentary on the fatal concepts of woman and love, science and pride, ameliorism and creative genius in modern times.

3. *Dialectic Transfer: The Idea in Action*

Both analogy and irony involve the transformation of one fictional identity into another. And Dante's specification of his method as "poetic, fictive, descriptive, digressive, transumptive; and likewise proceeding by definition, division, proof, refutation and setting forth of examples" is a good epigraph for much that our study of the modes of identification in allegory has detailed thus far. Another use of trope in allegory, implicit in Dante's statement, is the dialectic process. Here a general observation of Kenneth Burke's may help to make the connection:

A human role (such as we get in drama) may be summed up in certain slogans, or formulae, or epigrams, or "ideas" that characterize the agent's situation or strategy. The role involves properties both intrinsic to the agent and developed with relation to the scene and other agents. And the "summings-up" ("ideas") similarly possess properties derived both from the agent and from the various factors with which the agent is in relationship. Where the ideas are in action, we have drama; where the agents are in ideation, we have dialectic.[2]

The observation touches on what has been said about the use of irony and the naive central character in Swift and Kafka. The dialectic element, noted by Dante and Burke, is essential to allegory, where the process may be termed dialectic transfer. Dialectic transfer can be seen in allegory as the transvaluation of fictional agents from relatively static ideational figures at the start to progressively more active and meaningful roles in the course of the narrative. That is, through the devices we have discussed—emblem and talisman, nomenclatural symbol and allusion, and so forth—the attributes of characters are initially identified so that the reader gets some sense of the possibilities they may come to represent. The dialectic transfer is effected when their ideational roles are fully tested in the action (the "drama") and finally resolved in the larger design of the allegory.

A moral counterpart to this aspect of dialectic transfer shows up in D. H. Lawrence's remarks on Melville's picture of paradise among the Polynesian island cannibals. Lawrence says that the celebration of primitive rites on remote Typee appealed to Melville's narrator because the ceremony seemed to relieve him from the pressures of civilized society, until he found the underlying barbarism repugnant to his moral nature. Eating human flesh as against the symbolic eating of Christ's body, the life of indolence as against the life of purposeful activity, could no longer be regarded as questions inviting a free choice. The civilized man cannot abide bloody rites; they must at least be transubstantiated, morally transformed, if he is to retain his faith in the world and in himself. He cannot pretend he has gone back to Eden, as if Christ had never existed. And if he lives without faith in the allegory of Christ's birth and resurrection he must find some communion of equal efficacy to believe in. Otherwise he must do without the illusion of possessing a moral nature at all.

Dostoevski makes a similar point at the end of his short tale, *The Dream of a Ridiculous Man:* "The consciousness of life is higher than life, the knowledge of the laws of happiness is higher than happiness—that is what one must contend against." The moral imagination is a rare acquisition which grows painfully out of the defeats and perplexities of the affective life, the momentary exaltations of the personal ego, the temporary satisfactions and refuges which life accidentally and fitfully bestows. To discipline and fulfill these yearnings, fleetingly experienced and often thought synonymous with life itself, the moral imagination learns to incorporate them in everyday experience. For the power to be an individual, to be wholly oneself, is vested in the personal consciousness. The consciousness is biologically grounded, and conditioned by the environmental situation. It is also actively formed by many experiences which force one to look at oneself objectively. This capacity engages all one's personal talents and limitations, one's relations with others, one's sense of time and place, and so on. The growth and maturity of the individual consciousness, so highly prized by civilized men, are intangible and inexpressible progressions. But the values of a mature consciousness are expressible through the moral imagination, although typically in abstract terms whose defect is that they so easily become deadened and detached from the vitalizing symbolic forms which recurrently celebrate them.

In allegory, where the concepts of philosophy often merge

with the illusion-making of literary art, the moral imagination
imitates the growth of the individual consciousness within the
limiting, essentially tragic conditions of human existence. In
Burke's terms, the human role of the agent always includes, in
its identity and growth, the ideas elicited through its action.
Being at the same time both agent and idea, the human role is
fixed only when we abstract it from the narrative course. Its
being both tells us that it is serving an essential purpose of the
fiction which must be taken into account. The connection between drama and dialectic encompasses the imitation of life in
all its manifestations and the evaluative principle which gives
life, the particular and individual life of the agent, its meaning.
Thus dialectic transfer is the reciprocal evolving of agent and
idea within the dynamic movement of the fiction. Drama, moving slowly from within and issuing, as from a tight core, outward, manifests itself centrifugally, while dialectic moves inward, centripetally, from without. Hence the living quality of
the allegorical fiction is made up of alternating movements that
suggest the actual rhythm of living organisms.

We can see an instance of dialectic transfer at work by following briefly Ishmael's role in *Moby Dick*.

If not the hero of the novel, Ishmael is the author's mask, the
ideal voluntary witness, the *raisonneur*. Through him the purpose of the voyage is described, defined, and in some sense
proved. He prepares the drama by calling attention to his own
immediate situation—his initial "spleen," his chance encounter
with Queequeg, and his apparently haphazard drifting toward
"the overwhelming idea of the whale." But in noting his character and the underlying urgency which moves it, we begin to
sense something at work which is just the opposite of chance—
something dark, fateful, and predestined. As narrator of the
voyage he charts the *Pequod's* metaphysical and "non-acci-
dental" course while reporting on the ship's adventures and
navigational course. He also designates the dramatic function
of Ahab and the other characters, and at various points in the
narrative he distinguishes their ideational meaning in a dialec-

tic exposition. Through Ishmael's intermediacy, dialectic transfer occurs as a progressive sequence in the action which is seen
simultaneously on the levels of perception and judgment. But
as the author's persona during most of the novel Ishmael refracts
these meanings, as it were, through the limitations of his own
consciousness. And so it is essential to determine what he is
like and what impels him from the start.

At the beginning Ishmael decides to go to sea in order to cure
a temporary fit of despair. He seems at some pains to make it
clear that this is his main reason, and not that he shuns the society of other men. He reveals his own pride and excitement
in anticipating the voyage; but such emotions seem rationalized
when he indicates that he is doing only what most men, including the hypnotized group of water gazers on the Battery,
would like to do. In joining the crew he chooses a situation requiring greater restriction and social cooperation than any similar association on land. He would make his going to sea appear
innocent and no more misanthropic than following a common
urge to see the world. The sense is unmistakable, however,
that in shipping out he is abandoning the specified routine of
life on land for the unspecified allurements of life at sea. And
yet even the invitation of the sea and the mysterious idea of the
whale seem for him little more than feasible incentives. Ambivalence pervades his initial rationalizations and movements.
It is as if some unknown compulsion drives him; he cannot
seem to find a ship fast enough. On the other hand, he appears
acquiescent and compliant, even willing to loiter, once he enters the company of other mariners.

Coming into New Bedford at night, Ishmael passes up several inns—apprehensively rejected as being "too expensive and
jolly"—stumbles in and quickly out of a Negro church, and
finally puts up at a whaler's hostel, the Spouter-Inn, managed
by Peter Coffin. Here, in a painting on the wall, he unwittingly
observes emblematic foreshadowings of the *Pequod's* fate. Here
also, under the sign of Coffin, he meets the cannibal Queequeg,
whose coffin is later to serve him as a life-raft when he becomes

the *Pequod's* sole survivor. And here, lastly, doing what most men would do "if they but knew it," Ishmael becomes the cannibal's soul-mate. On his knees beside Queequeg, he worships the little wooden idol in purest Christian charity. The act confirms Father Mapple's sentence, from a sermon which is still fresh in Ishmael's mind: "And if we obey God, we must disobey ourselves; and it is in this disobeying ourselves, wherein the hardness of obeying God consists." Kneeling with Queequeg, he seems to be parodying the sermon; but his jocose rationalization is tempered by a penetrating syllogism:

I was a good Christian; born and bred in the bosom of the infallible Presbyterian Church. How then could I unite with this wild idolator in worshipping his piece of wood? But what is worship? thought I. Do you suppose now, Ishmael, that the magnanimous God of heaven and earth—pagans and all included—can possibly be jealous of an insignificant bit of black wood? Impossible! But what is worship?—to do the will of God—*that* is worship. And what is the will of God?—to do to my fellow man what I would have my fellow man do to me—*that* is the will of God. Now, Queequeg is my fellow man. And what do I wish that this Queequeg would do to me? Why, unite with me in my particular form of worship. Consequently, I must then unite with him in his; ergo, I must turn idolator.

The statement is echoed soon afterward when Queequeg saves an insolent passenger from drowning on the way over to Nantucket and then appears "to be saying to himself—'It's a mutual, joint-stock world, in all meridians. We cannibals must help these Christians.'" It is re-echoed, we realize at the end, when Ishmael is himself saved by means of Queequeg's coffin; and thereby Ishmael's humanity, the virtue which makes him worth saving, comes to be rewarded. Ishmael's virtue develops from his discovery and enactment of human fellowship throughout the voyage in contrary motion to his original impulses as an "isolato," the social outcast of Biblical reference designated in his name. It is this virtue that distinguishes him from the others—from Ahab's unavailing audacity, "the incompetence of mere unaided virtue . . . in Starbuck, the invulnerable jollity of indifference in Stubb, and the pervading mediocrity in Flask." In the light of this differentiation, and because Ishmael can grow and learn, his apparently random decision to go to sea turns into a moral venture where his role is to transform actions into ideas and ideas into actions.

Ishmael continually deepens the meaning of the voyage. His growing recognition of purpose knits the visible world together by the force of love and fellowship—a centrifugal force which is exhibited in a constant multiplication of analogies. The opposite effect, in Ahab's case—a condensation and concentration of purpose—proceeds simultaneously in a centripetal direction so that the hunt of the whale becomes a hunt after absolute truth, a purblind pursuit of the unattainable. This sinuous dialectical interplay between actions and ideas, between the movement outward and the movement inward, is climaxed in Ishmael's ruminations on the whiteness of the whale "that above all things appalled me."

As a rational man he tries to understand the white mystery by comparing it with all conceivable instances of whiteness in nature, history, and myth. But with the white whale as his inescapable referent, he finds each instance turning into an image of duplicity; so that "symbolize whatever grand or gracious thing he will by whiteness, no man can deny that in its profoundest idealized significance it calls up a peculiar apparition to the soul." A metaphysical duality divides the world: "In many of its aspects this visible world seems formed in love," and "the invisible spheres were formed in fright." This leads Ishmael to the question which the whole book dramatizes in Ahab's obsession—why whiteness "is at once the most meaning symbol of spiritual things, nay, the very veil of the Christian's Deity; and yet should be as it is, the intensifying agent in things the most appalling to mankind?" The reply is contained in the famous passage ending with the sentence, "Wonder ye then at the fiery hunt?"

The white whale is driven inward, as it were, to become a symbol for all creation; it contains the purpose, vanity, and

eternal blandishments of all answers to the question of existence. It represents, not the Deity, but the enigma which the
Deity has propounded and shaped in the gigantic physical
form of the white whale. Because Ishmael perceives this, he
alone is redeemed from the nightmare hunt after absolute
whiteness, and is released from the vortex of appearance that
has swallowed the *Pequod* and its crew. It is appropriate that
in *The Confidence Man* Ishmael's counterpart and successor
should appear, journeying downriver in mid-continental America, disguised as the apostle of light, a sun god; for his masquerade is an ironic response to Ishmael's need to operate
within the medium of colors upon matter so as not to "touch
all objects . . . with its own blank tinge."

There are similar if less probing instances of dialectic transfer in *The Scarlet Letter*. There it turns upon the insistent trans-
formative power of Hester's letter, affecting other characters besides herself, as well as all of nature. But to the degree that
Hawthorne's fiction holds fast to the Christian formula of original sin, it moves more on the ideational plane than on the dramatic. His characters, as if hypnotized by a masterful hand,
seem to act out some dream of purpose from which the full glow
of reality and self-determination has faded. *Moby Dick*, moving
simultaneously on both planes, meets the metaphysical problem
head on, and the impact yields as comprehensive a definition
of phenomenal reality as it is possible to get in allegory: a
reality that is both contained in its own manifest self-sufficiency
and fluid and chanceful as the sea. It is neither predetermined
nor paraphrasable in any formula. The esthetic and moral dimensions of the fiction come together in a vision of natural
continuity. At the end of *Moby Dick* nature's inexhaustible
cycle is represented, "and the great shroud of the sea rolled on
as it rolled five thousand years ago" at the Creation. Having
risen out of the "slowly wheeling circle," in the wake of the
drowned *Pequod*, Ishmael bobs up, as from a "vital center,"
like a new Adam on the face of the unknown. At such points
Melville's vision of the eternal confluence of man with nature

suggests Dante's vision of a similar transcendence at the end
of the Paradiso:

> But like to a wheel whose circling nothing jars
> Already on my desire and will prevailed
> The love that moves the sun and the other stars.
> (tr. Laurence Binyon)

The triumph of the allegorical method in Melville and Dante
is that the vision of each is embodied and effected through the
transmutation of the narrator's ideational role into a dramatic
human role. In such a way the world is thoroughly remade
without any violation of its physical and historical forms.
Quickened by what exists in actuality and by what is totally
conceivable between paradise lost and paradise regained, the
creative vision fulfills the ideal by transforming it into a universal experience of the real.

VI
The Ideal

We were fashioned to live in Paradise, and Paradise was destined to serve us. Our destiny has been altered; that this has also happened with the destiny of Paradise is not stated.

FRANZ KAFKA, *Aphorisms*

In behalf of the dignity of whaling, I would advance nought but substantiated facts.

HERMAN MELVILLE, *Moby Dick*

I took a second leave of my master; but as I was going to prostrate myself to kiss his hoof, he did me the honour to raise it gently to my mouth. I am not ignorant how much I have been censured for mentioning this last particular. For my detractors are pleased to think it improbable that so illustrious a person should descend to give so great a mark of distinction to a creature so inferior as I. Neither have I forgot how apt some travellers are to boast of extraordinary favours they have received. But if these censurers were better acquainted with the noble and courteous disposition of the Houyhnhnms, they would soon change their opinion.

JONATHAN SWIFT, *Gulliver's Travels*

In LIFE as in literature, ideals generally issue from the tendency to visualize a state of uninterrupted happiness or perfection; these images are shaped upon the past or future so that the memory or anticipation of such a state is localized in time. A primitive form of the ideal appears in fantasies and dreams as something imagistically or dramatically ready-made. In more sophisticated forms, as in the philosophic or scientific pursuits of first principles and causality, the ideal gets rationalized and eventually expressed by means of conceptual or mathematical systems.

Psychologists tell us that in fantasies and dreams the psyche seeks to renew, or to provide some substitute for, an early harmony experienced in infancy. This harmony is a state of instinct gratification felt before the need to adapt to reality has intervened in the consciousness. The ego, we are told, is the assertive and synthesizing force of the personality developing out of the id—all the inarticulate, instinctual urges. When the individual gradually wakes up to the world of adult authority, his images of his outer world are incorporated as his superego. The ego's conservative nature then compels it to reconcile the instinctual needs of the id with the qualifying adjurations of the superego. Whenever these attempts fail, the unconscious creates dramatic images of repression or substitutive images of success.

Since this tendency to try to recover an earlier harmony is apparently innate to both the conscious and unconscious parts of the psyche, it may be related, according to Freud, to basic physiological phenomena. Freud speculates on the connection between the compulsive character of the instinct and the recapitulative function of organisms:

It seems, then, that an instinct is a compulsion inherent in organic life to restore an earlier state of things which the living entity has been obliged to abandon under the pressure of external disturbing forces; that is, it is a kind of organic elasticity, or, to put it another way, the expression of inertia inherent in organic life. . . . We see how the germ of a living animal is obliged in the course of its development to recapitulate (even if only in a transient and abbreviated fashion) the structures of all the forms from which it is sprung, instead of proceeding quickly by the shortest path to its final shape. . . . So too, the power of regenerating a lost organ by growing afresh a precisely similar one, extends far up into the animal kingdom.[1]

By implication Freud's conclusion, "that everything living dies for *internal* reasons—becomes inorganic once again" (that is, finds its death appropriately), illuminates a strongly determining aspect of the ideal:

Every modification which is thus imposed upon the course of the organism's life is accepted by the conservative organic instincts and stored up for further repetition. Those instincts are therefore bound to give a deceptive appearance of being forces tending towards change and progress, whilst in fact they are merely seeking to reach an ancient goal by paths alike old and new. Moreover it is possible to specify this final goal of all organic striving. It would be in contradiction to the conservative nature of the instincts if the goal of life were a state of things which had never yet been attained. On the contrary, it must be an old state of things, an initial state from which the living entity has at one time or other departed and to which it is striving to return by circuitous paths along which its development leads.[2]

Here the paradox—that one looks backward while going forward (developing), and conversely, that one goes backward (toward death) while looking forward—derives from the dynamic role of *eros*, the life force moving inexorably toward a conclusion which reflects its beginnings. Freud's observation concurs with many ancient beliefs about the cyclic nature of existence, particularly with theories of metempsychosis and with the Heraclitean view that "the way up and the way down are the same." It also recalls the deterministic principles of Christian analogy dominated by the anagoge (the ideal of purpose), and the medieval conception of hierarchy (the chain of being), to which those principles are allied.

Christian analogy lays stress on an "eternal present" subsuming the living and the dead and vouchsafed by the instrumentality of divine will in all existence. The divine will is vested in the anagoge, the issue of heavenly justice and rewards, whereby all created beings tend to find their ultimate forms. In addition, the moral and social order—since Christian analogy is also concerned with justifying behavior according to divine law—is implemented by an evaluative hierarchy, a great chain of being. "According to this conception," as one commentator puts it,

> . . . degrees of value are objectively present in the universe. Everything except God has some natural superior; everything except unformed matter has some natural inferior. The goodness, happiness, and dignity of every being consists in obeying its natural superior and ruling its natural inferiors. . . . Every being is a conductor of superior love or *agape* to the being below it, and of inferior love or *eros* to the being above. Such is the loving inequality between the intelligence who guides a sphere and the sphere which is guided.[3]

In this view *eros* and *agape* explain the human capacity that keeps the world together, while at the same time upholding the distinctions between subhuman species and between social classes. Behind the Christian view is an ideal of moral and social behavior which emphasizes the injunction to love as a right and duty. But Christian *eros* is not of course the instinctual life force it is for Freud; it is love that takes its pattern from the divine work of creation in Genesis, and looks forward to divine justice by stipulating "natural" inequality and obedience as self-evident tenets of human law. In urging acquiescence in the Gospel idea of man fallen through disobedience and redeemed through Christ's love, the other aspect of love, *agape*, becomes an imitation of divine love and prescribes how man may regain his lost paradise. This transcendent ideal of *eros* and *agape* encompasses all human behavior, and dominates the fourfold method of Christian analogy. The spiritual or parabolic sense, prefigured in the literal (God's word, the event), includes the allegorical (the meaning according to belief), the tropological (the meaning according to duty), and the anagogical (the meaning according to the divine tendency of the event). These conceptions are summarized in the scholastic aphorism: *"Litera gesta docet; quid credas allegoria;/Moralis quid agas; quo tendas anagogia."* By itself the anagoge stands for the ideal reality, the highest meanings; as a component part of a total allegory it rounds out the purpose of all events—historical, moral, political, and social—thus identifying the nature of all being and declaring what existence is for.

This ideal sense of over-all purpose, the anagoge, becomes dissociated from the other senses in later developments of literary allegory when the hierarchic concept and the whole cosmic view of Christian analogy break down. The ideal then appears in various forms: as an implied norm from which men have strayed (particularly in satire); as a desired good to which men need to be converted, and hence allied to some social, political, or religious idea (often in allegory and pastoral); as an unattainable state of past or future perfection, and consequently a judicial principle by which everything mundane is measured (in all types of symbolic fiction, including the epic). In these versions the ideal gauges the spiritual or psychological distance that men have fallen. The task of the hero, whose career is made to cover this distance, is obviously to pick up clues and find a way out of the predicament by exploring the realm that separates the earthly from the divine, or to insist on seeking "the true way," however unattainable it is.

Upon the gradual dissociation of the anagoge from the other levels of meaning, a vigorous reformation of the ideal begins. The world of reality becomes a fabulous appearance which needs testing by an heroic consciousness that has dispensed with the old answers and the old keys. The literary work increasingly strives to create its own sufficiency as a form. Thereupon the symbolism of the quest turns on the dialectic play between perception and conception—as, for instance, through the delusion of size and its importance in *Gulliver* and *Moby Dick*, and through the ambiguity of values Kafka gives to distance and proximity. Various philosophical formulas support and reflect the rephrasing of esthetic questions concerning life and art, history and poetry, comedy and tragedy; these include Renaissance Neoplatonism, Kant's categorical imperative, German transcendental idealism, Goethe's Eternal Feminine, Kierkegaard's existentialism, Freud's id-ego-superego triad, and so on. As this rephrasing process continues, symbolic fiction pushes out into several more or less distinct types. In retrospect it becomes possible to think of allegory, pastoral, satire, and epic as types in which generic and stylistic elements are compounded, and as differing principally in their treatment and localization of the ideal. As a strictly esthetic quality, however, the dominant ideal in these types is identified with the organic purpose variously fulfilled in the works themselves—that is, with the total consummation of artistic aim and design.

As the Protestant ethic comes to bloom new literary forms proliferate and monotypical precepts in art gradually break up. It then becomes difficult to conceive of literary forms as lending themselves to any pure and simple typology. And so with allegory, as most specimens since Dante show: the literary type comes to be shaped by the impression which certain thematic ideas have enforced upon it and by the various literary forms to which it has been adapted. Moreover, what seems to characterize its moral emphasis, modes of identification, and narrative procedure often obtains as well for epic, satire, and pastoral. All these types employ tropes as basic units of symbolic directives and fictional extension. The types are further related in that they all depict a metaphysical view or a social bias toward the verities of contemporary experience. And such effects seem to impress themselves upon the symbolic types more than any literary prescription or the inherited usages of a literary form.

Of course, one may often translate into ideas a symbolic development in fiction, or trace back to an earlier source a convention of thematic treatment. For instance, the case for Hester Prynne and Dimmesdale against Chillingworth in *The Scarlet Letter* has been summarized by F. O. Matthiessen in the Calvinistic doctrine "that excessive love for things which should take only a secondary place in the affections, though tending to the sin of lust, is less grave than love distorted, love turned from God and from his creatures, into self-consuming envy and vengeful pride." [4] This "translation" helps deepen one's sense of the novel's historical dimension. It also suggests how closely the doctrine in the novel accords with the medieval hierarchic view of life which frames one aspect of the moral law as Hawthorne saw it. One might profit similarly by tracing the descent of obscenity in the Italian pastoral from the Orphic original, and Satan's Miltonic heroism from the Homeric gods.

But no investigation of this sort is likely to account for the generic qualities we call allegorical, pastoral, or epical in specific works. These qualities are more directly attributable to the uniquely personal projections the individual writer creates. It is through the successive fulfillments of many such writers that the types develop and change; it is also true that because certain classic examples treat similar ideas we habitually think of them as belonging to a distinct type. But the whole question of how far one may go in identifying a work with a specific literary type remains indeterminate since it involves making a metonymic reduction—that is, finding the difference in similar materials and the similarity in different materials—which itself presupposes some hypothesis about what constitutes the type.

Typology is nevertheless an invaluable critical resource because it helps one discern common literary structures in many works, which would otherwise elude one's scrutiny of the individual work. But one must deal flexibly with the types, remembering that the conceptual elements in typology are antedated by the fictional works themselves. Typology provides a generalized framework for appraising characteristic relationships among different works, not legislative acts to which the works must be made to conform.

Even the barest survey of the symbolic types indicates that, far from being a set of rigid theoretical codifications, they are useful because richly adaptable to various literary embodiments. In this way their history helps to reveal a great deal about the social and ethical interests that subsist in these embodiments. Such a survey broadens the base from which to observe the workings of allegory. It also shows how the methods of allegory lend themselves to other fictions that speak its cosmic language and mirror its symbolic design.

1. *Epic: The Hero and His Cultural Burden*

In relating the epic to the customs of the Homeric age, one historian points to the flexibility of the hero's association with other characters. The hero is a gentleman of superior judgment and skill. Such endowments make him a leader of men—a captain, governor, judge, and pioneer adventurer. He is not a tyrant but a companion to those who serve him and share in his enterprises. A sort of aristocrat with a distinctly democratic temperament, he enacts the principle of *noblesse oblige*. Outfitting his own ship, carrying his men along by force of his own ideas, purposes, and character, he needs no discipline other than his own. His ambition and knowledge guide him; those who follow him do so unquestioningly as his fellows, the partakers and supporters of his mission, but also as his social inferiors.[5]

These generalizations define the position and character of Homer's Ulysses. They also touch on the situation of Captain Ahab, the heroic adventurer of a much later age. But if both these figures and their times may be called heroic, the parallel serves only to set off the cultural and psychological differences which make Ahab so incongruous an epic hero when placed alongside Ulysses. Ulysses' famous guile is evidently a dominant personal trait, but it is also an attribute necessary for heroic mastery in a seafaring venture contrived mainly to test fortitude and patience during a twenty-year voyage. His trait is so effectively portrayed that we associate craftiness and ingenuity not only with Ulysses' name and story but also with the virtues most prized by his age. Ahab's pride and single-mindedness are qualities of a more ambiguous coloring. They are fostered by a time when whaling was among America's principal industries, and when a strong, even tyrannical, hand was invaluable to a captain whose crew was usually ill-assorted and irresponsible, if not mutinous. But in the novel Ahab's traits take a rather different turn. In his pursuit of one whale, pride and single-mindedness turn into ruthlessness and blasphemy, the darker consequences of an individualism highly favored by Romantic and mercantile ethics alike. It is the transformation of Ahab's actions in the crucible of his intense single need, so that they finally subjugate practical motives, that relates him to the heroism of an age as legendary as Homer's.

Such a comparison, then, would provide clues for answering the question: What happens to change the classic conception of the hero as a figure invested with heroism by virtue of his birth, vocation, and affiliation to some class ideal? A complete answer would have to take into account the hero's individual problems; it would have to identify the critical situation of his culture as well as the predicament of all heroes when looked at as successors to powerful legendary or historical figures who have explored the way before.

In the full light of its cultural expression, any single epic undoubtedly rehearses those attributes the hero has in common with all other heroes. Kenneth Burke's speculations on the subject cut across historical differences and account for the epic hero as a recurrent configuration of cultural processes. A charismatic leader of men, the epic hero, according to Burke, is one who magnifies and makes socially acceptable the actual conditions of men living under stress or in primitive conditions. The hero is a repository for all the virtues the group needs to believe in to survive. Other men live vicariously in his deeds, his courage, and self-sacrifice, and thus share in a communion (or community), both social and religious, of the heroic body. The mediator between men and gods, the epic hero humanizes divinity by his flaws and sufferings no less than by his miraculous exploits. In identifying with these heroes other men come to see in themselves the same predisposition to persecute and suffer as well as the means for ennobling their fateful human condition. And this, "the invitation to seek the flaw in oneself," Burke concludes, "promotes in the end the attitude of *resignation* which, when backed by *well-rounded* symbolic structure, is nothing other than the inventory of one's personal limits." [6]

The epic hero, then, like the hero in other symbolic types, invariably becomes a didactic figure for the reader. Even very different heroes like Bunyan's Christian and Kafka's K. elicit in their respective periods similar responses from readers who need to oppose or become identified with a prevalent incarnation of authority. It is by this power in the hero to call forth such responses that we can gauge his archetypicality. Going beyond the "attitude of resignation" in the hero, one finds instances of heroes in whom an acquiescence to the fact of a personal flaw frees them from the paralyzing struggle for perfection. Against threats of self-doubt, the recognition of a flaw actually promotes triumph over resignation by enabling such heroes to contend, on the basis of "election" or self-knowledge, with the demands and possibilities of experience.

With the heroic aspect of the epic's authority goes the historical, mythological, or doctrinal data it usually conveys, something that may strike later readers as being only so much excess baggage. But it is such baggage that gives the cultural evidence from which the epic grows. For the epic hero not only concentrates in himself prevalent but diffusely felt ideals —ideals which may have appeared only at random in pictorial art or in certain actual political careers—but in his encounters with antagonistic powers he also coordinates practical knowledge, technical facts, and theoretical possibilities not yet expressed in written form.

This documentary property of the epic persists in the evolution of the type down to our own day. It is displayed in all the cultural data and erudition worked into the narrative design. Because the erudition is frequently so compendious, armies of commentators subsequently extend it until the work is perpetuated as a storehouse of beliefs, a museum of iconographic relics. And so although the *Iliad* is a tale of daylight combat celebrating the vital efforts of consciousness, and *Moby Dick*—to an even greater degree, *Finnegans Wake*—is a tale which penetrates the powers of irrational addictions, the documentation in both reveals as much about the differences between ancient and modern cultures as the imagery and diction reveal about the typical prepossessions of the two periods.

2. *Satire: The Heroic Dethroned*

Like allegory, satire serves at times as a rhetorical mode, and like allegory and epic it often appears as a full-fledged literary form. Criticism usually puts satire opposite to allegory and epic, just as comedy is traditionally put opposite to tragedy. It has been shown that satire becomes allegorical in centralizing a dominant ideal by means of irony and analogy; and in the best of Swift and Kafka, where the distinctive devices of both allegory and satire surcharge an almost inexpressible complexity of view, it becomes impossible to distinguish between the types. But the specific values of satire are, of course, always double-edged. In dethroning the epic hero and questioning the active virtues which modeled him, satire appears heretical or iconoclastic. But, in attempting to revitalize ideals from which society is pulling away, satire reveals its essentially conservative bias. Defects in the epic hero are discovered and magnified; and the exposure is made to undermine all contemporaneous forms of heroism. But the undercover means of effecting the distortion in satire are the same means by which something of the authority and values of heroic times—an otherwise forgotten Golden Age—is dramatically reinvoked. Such typical transformations are achieved in Swift and Kafka. But the ludicrous distortion of isolated defects we call caricature is not what Swift and Kafka aim at. For one thing, their distortions usually are far from being funny; for another, they exhibit not the isolated but the fundamental moral defects of all men living in society. How fundamental the defects are—or even that they exist—we seldom realize until we scrutinize them realistically, without vanity or other illusions. When we do examine them closely, the experience is so discomforting as to appear wholly monstrous—which is the very effect of Swift's and Kafka's distortions.

The moral realist—an agnomen of every satirist—sees a world drained of color and objective truth. There, every motive and action has some factitious aspect; and there, everybody pretends that this is not so, but even if they had to admit it were so they would certainly not blame themselves. Moral realism becomes synonymous with the realization that what the senses and the judgment report to each other suffers from the equivocations of both. And since we obviously cannot judge without our physical perceptions, one way to emphasize the pathetic interdependency is to exaggerate the claims of the perceptual upon the judicial.

This hoaxed equation is typical in Swiftian satire. A shift in perception stipulates a shift in judgment. Thus the deformities Gulliver perceives in the skin blemishes and body odors of the Brobdingnagians seem to result from his greater physical sensitivity, his acuter sensory apparatus. But being so small and delicate has its compensations; it causes the giants to treat him as a pet so that he begins to imagine he is exceptional—a valiant fighter of flies and mice, and a counselor to the king—instead of the freak pigmy he actually is. His mistaken pride arises from the fact of his puniness; he sees only that which, in distinguishing him, will be useful to him and thus compensate for his defects, out of which he must continually make some virtue.

Gulliver's perception in Brobdingnag is of course the reverse of a similar abnormality in perception in Lilliput; but the same mistaken pride involves him in its ironies. For there, as a short-sighted giant, Gulliver has the piquant illusion that the Lilliputians are exquisitely well-proportioned creatures. By the same token he is prevented from understanding how his own disproportionate attributes and functions constantly offend the natives. But while the Brobdingnagians and Lilliputians are in physical and other respects still comparable to humanity elsewhere, the abhorrent animality of the Yahoos, especially as contrasted with the reasonableness of horses, the beguiling Houyhnhnms, permanently dislocates Gulliver's sensibility on his return to normal humanity at home. Presumably he can no longer relate his faulty perception to his faulty judgment. So Gulliver's voyages are a cumulative experience leading to the realization, again and again, that deformity—the flaw—is the normal condition of man. The external deformity has revealed a corresponding moral deformity in all men and in himself. Although it follows that the great gap between everyday illusion and reality can be made clear only through the delusive reports of the senses, it seems equally true that this is the gap into which one must necessarily fall. Thus Gulliver's isolation at the end represents the fallen condition of all mankind.

In Kafka's novels systematic distortions of the real world correspond almost biologically with the rhythm of the hero's shifting relations to it. Periods of intense magnification, of clairvoyant perceptions, when the whole picture is steadily beheld with dismaying clarity, alternate with periods of sluggish, will-less myopia when objects are lost in a haze, and only the throbbing of a vein in his neck reminds the hero he is still alive. Kafka's heroes keep searching for their identity in an order of reality that has not yet disclosed itself. They appear on the scene after some surrender to darkness, following an indescribable loss—whether of childhood, a friend, or a good job. They arrive full of a desperate and astonished urgency, seeking to concentrate rationality and will, effort and hope, in a single task which they feel will effect their reinstatement in the fallen world that is now their real world.

At first this world, which they have entered so late, seems to promise them a place or at least some marginal status. But thereafter the identification of objects and persons and all basic human relationships, so necessary to understand before anything can be done, constantly shift, impelling new loyalties and strategies which inevitably lead away from the main purpose. Like retarded children they seem to be engaged in the first stages of a process which others have passed through long before. Progress is illusory, however—existing only when some strategy seems more effective than another at a particular moment. In the long run it becomes impossible to conceive of moving in any direction, and all effort turns into the chilling proof of Zeno's paradox. Burdened by their acute but mistaken rationality, Kafka's heroes cannot cope with the fallen world, the world of other men's experience, which they can never take for granted. This situation is another version of the problem dealt with in *The Confidence Man*—that of having somehow to support the illusion against the reality: untenable though the illusion may be, there is no alternative. For the positive world endures against the proof of its own irrationality, which is shown in the failure of the hero. As Melville in *Pierre* puts the idea: "For in tremendous extremities human souls are like drowning men; well enough they know they are in peril; well enough they know the causes of that peril; nevertheless the sea is the sea, and these drowning men do drown." And similarly in *The Trial* Kafka's K. says, "What is laid on us is to accomplish the negative—the positive is already given." Nevertheless in Kafka it is this world that is on trial, with its superstitious worship of bureaucracy and its inert irrationality which the hero attempts to understand; but its nature is inexorably to defeat him just when he is about to receive some revelation that would have done him no good even if he had succeeded in receiving it. The guardians of the law, the castle, the father, the advocates are not to blame, but rather the injunctions of disused authority, blinder than the hero's myopia, more unyielding than his futile clairvoyance. The guardians are after all only the agents of fallen reality—which is what the distortions of satire make evident. It is on this ground that the ethical implications of satiric art seem to emerge most vividly.

The study of art is the study of hesitations in form; its counterpart is the study of ethics, the study of man's hesitations in society. The satirist, in whose biases the two are merged, has understood the ancient virtues—the good, the true, and the beautiful; friendship, love, and magnanimity; concord among individuals, family, town, and the state. One might say that for Kafka they are precisely the values upon which happiness must be staked. Yet in Kafka the virtues fail in action, in individual experience, because they are not naturally operative but contradictory and oppressive, not just but arbitrary. They do not ennoble, they help to degrade. They are not benevolent or truly instructive, they are authoritarian. The free man is not distinguishable from the slave of custom; the stranger is still a misfit, an enemy of the state. The satirist's hero—explorer, salesman, surveyor, or clerk—is an anonymous representative of cultural gifts, the gifts of subservient mediocrity; he is distinguished only by his endless search for identity, for the meaning of individuality. In this situation the more extensive his search the more it is fated to drop behind its starting point, at last turning into an infinite regress towards inanition and death.

The defects in heroism on which satire seizes show up in the plight of the doomed and undistinguished hero, and in the ambiguity of his perspective. His equivocal sense of distance-in-proximity (and of its converse) relative to his goal, results from the hero's diminished understanding of freedom and his excessive feeling for necessity—a lack and a contingency which nevertheless permit him to go on. This central imbalance or distortion in him makes relative the absolute nature of his quest; but it also makes absolute the minor obstacles along the way, and thus mirrors the inexhaustibly circuitous character of the quest that confronts an undisclosable moral law. It is as if the flaw which humanizes the hero (makes him like everybody else) is merely the sum of all the defects of men living in organized society. So far as he represents this generalized flaw, he is able to get along in life; but so far as he is marked off by his urgent discontent, all his experiences add up to the reverse of resignation—the message of epic—making him a godlike or childlike explorer who is distinctly ill at ease in a world of easy acceptance. Instead of being an assertive and brilliant warrior, like the epic hero, he exhibits his uneasiness through vicious struggles with the self.

One concludes that the working formula in satire is just the reverse of that in epic, which serves to vivify and rationalize man's view of his own inadequacy by showing the flaws in gods. Satire dispenses with the gods and their standards and entirely demolishes man's image of himself as a rational creature. The world turns so drably familiar that the satiric hero can no longer tolerate resignation. Yet the world's appalling resignation adheres residually to the hero's consciousness, so that at various points in the struggle he is engulfed, perhaps mercifully, by it. Otherwise Kafka's heroes go on struggling desperately, believing that the generalized flaw is "out there," in the world, perhaps because they suspect finally that it is all too evident in themselves. In such ways the satiric hero dramatizes the terms in which doubt ravages the individual conscience, magnifying limited virtues and minimizing gross defects.

3. *Pastoral: Resurrection of Lost Paradises*

The traditional aim of pastoral, as of satire, is essentially serious: to contemporize an Eden, an Arcadia, a drowned Atlantis, or to bring back the vanished playground of innocence and childhood. Principally, it is to resurrect a lost paradise and invest it with new values. But since this particular treatment of the ideal is so easily mismanaged, pastoral seems to survive typically in what has been called an artificial "atmosphere of paradox and incongruity." Like allegory, it is known mainly by debased examples, the issue of fashionable Renaissance courts and colleges of manners.

It is characteristic of the artificiality of pastoral as a literary form that the impulse which gave the first creative touch at seeding loses itself later and finds no place among the forces at work at blossom time; the methods adopted by the greatest masters of the form are inconsistent with the motives that impelled them to their logical conclusion; the result, both in literature and in life, became a by-word for absurd unreality.[7]

But one way to keep pastoral alive after a literary plague has devitalized it is to mock its ideals openly; another way is to refurbish the pastoral form and renew traditional themes. Either way requires a strong sense of commitment to circumstances of living actuality and the creation of a new esthetic.

William Empson finds the second solution at work in the double plot of Elizabethan drama. There, both comic and serious elements were purged and eventually counterweighted and merged with one another, as in the Bottom-Theseus plots in *A Midsummer Night's Dream* or the Ariel-Caliban plots dominated by Prospero in *The Tempest*. According to Empson, the double plot provides a mechanism for promoting the ethical ideas that are synonymous with pastoral. The tragicomedy unites heroic and pastoral myths, which are salutary and basic to the needs of society. The other solution is evident in the mock-heroic style of certain picaresque novels where a natural liaison between epic and pastoral is set up before they are both parodied. What escapes parody in such novels are the social conventions of epic and pastoral: the distinctions between classes and the love of one class for the other or of one sex for the other. A good example, Empson continues, is *Don Quixote:*

One cause of the range of *Don Quixote*, the skyline beyond skyline of its irony, is that though mock-heroic it is straight pastoral; only at the second level, rather as the heroic becomes genuine, does the pastoral become mock. Most of the story ('oh basilisk of our mountains') might be taking place in Sydney's *Arcadia*, and as Quixote himself points out (I. IV. xxiii, in favour of the boy who was on graceful terms with his goat) the two conventions are alike, so that the book puzzles us between them; we cannot think one fatuous and not the other. A large fraction of it ignores Quixote while the characters tell romantic tales that partake of both; only slightly less romantic tales are part of the main story, and some of the ladies he absurdly fails to help (e.g., Dorothea, I. IV. ii) are actually in need of the sort of help he offers. This makes the satire seem more important by making his heroism less unreal, as do the cautiously implied comparisons of him with Christ, which make him the fool who becomes the judge.[8]

Empson's illustrations convincingly show that the new forms of dramatic irony and satire in the hands of Shakespeare and Cervantes succeeded in resurrecting ideals that had been condemned to pedantry and dilettantism.

Apparently the esthetic question concerning pastoral is subsumed under social and ethical matters which invariably attend upon the literary type. Pastoral dictates an idealized behavior that is protected from disillusioning consequences in the everyday world, while insisting upon its own standards as feasible, because imaginable and practicable, in the same world. Its tone and bias defy the fragmentations of everyday experience, and yet its examples—that is, specific events and the realistic behavior of people among the different classes— are covertly drawn from the world of contemporary actuality. Pastoral tries to show, as it were, how much brighter and hotter light may be when enclosed in a vacuum, and demands the same intensity of brightness and heat for the light existing outside the vacuum. It is a literature of recipe, which in part explains its attractiveness. It appeals to everyone who recognizes from his own experience the ingredients of which the recipe is composed—the discerning attitude of precocious children and misfit idealists, the wisdom of the poor and homely, the joys of the simple life, and the spontaneous expression of the passions between lovers. In this way it takes on a distinct social value. We all yearn for what we can imagine, even though it is unattainable. But how much more can we be made to want what is presented as possibly attainable after all!

Pastoral subsists in the practicability of its ideals and in its pointed criticism of all social behavior that falsifies or inhibits these ideals. In later examples of pastoral, the typical mock-heroics resound with deeper seriousness. The quixotism of Barnaby Rudge or Prince Mishkin raises the judicial principle above the shambles of hypocritical creeds. Also, in *Huckleberry Finn* or in the pastoral novels of Lawrence, Forster, and Conrad we find something more vital than the old back-to-nature formula or the blithe inducement to consort with shepherds or savages; we discover a criticism of civilized society's inability to produce an integrated individual, let alone a universal hero.

The critical attitude is made explicit in the typical Lawrence, Forster, or Conrad novel; there the hero is put into a situation which shows an idyllic surpassing of real-life adversity within credible naturalistic surroundings. The hero's uncompromising nature challenges the heavy-footed class determinism or the sentimental amorality shackling the other characters. His superiority is especially evident when the hero's companion lacks his idyllic qualities and he is thus raised to the condition of being "vitally alone." The hero (or heroine) then serves mainly to urge other characters into a stricter awareness of themselves or to enact for them broader possibilities of self-realization. The hero becomes a case in point by overcoming the holocaust of a narrow determinism to which other characters succumb. D. H. Lawrence's *White Peacock* and *Women in Love* illustrate some of these general observations.

The pastoral elements in *The White Peacock* involve an unhappy crossing of classes and lovers against a landscape of perennial natural beauty. Always lowering, like the threat of a bad winter, is the society outside—the striking miners, the poachers, the evil squire, and his gamekeeper. The gamekeeper is a consistently fatalistic creature, who dies according to his own shallow determinism. On another level there is the romantic fatalism of George Saxton, who drinks himself to death. One is made to feel more particularly that George fails because he did not recognize a conviction of his own nature, which was to act when Lettie, his beloved, was ready to have him. In violating his own nature he violates the natural order. Thereafter, and as if in consequence, Lettie lapses into an unloving hollow sort of motherhood because she has accepted Leslie, the squire, instead of George. The gamekeeper is the unfulfilled noble savage, and George, the natural but weak aristocrat; Leslie represents the hardened remnant of an aristocracy that has lost its benevolent hold on society, and Lettie is the bluestocking whose "education" misguides her instincts. Because of sexual restraints, preconceived obligations to class, and betrayal of their basic nature, the inability of the characters to get along together becomes the reverberant moral note in the novel. And yet, though this approach to their relationships is nothing if not serious, one senses in it the constant encroachment of ludicrous forces that threaten to turn the novel into a sentimental melodrama.

In *Women in Love*, which concerns the problems of sexuality in love and friendship, Lawrence treats the pastoral elements more complexly. The first half of the novel wanders uncertainly as motives are planted among the characters. But beginning with the second half, minor characters and naturalistic preoccupations are discarded. Lawrence fastens on the relationship between two couples (Ursula and Birkin; Gudrun and Crich), and moves the narrative out of the tediously elaborated theme of isolation into a quickened sense of struggle and doom, where the strength of personal identity is constantly attacked by the passions. Basic to this interest is the impasse the sisters, Ursula and Gudrun, create for their lovers, who consequently are forced into a close but ambiguous comradeship. There is no conventional hero among them; they are four violent forces of psychic appetite. Birkin wants love, but more than love a contact without commitment; he wants the possibility of love with one desirable woman and one desirable man. This he fails to achieve. He stands opposed, therefore, to Crich's negative animality just as Ursula, in her desire for full possession, stands opposed to Gudrun's passive narcissism. For Gudrun there is no limit except in her own helpless return to cruelty and sadism. For Ursula the limit is Birkin's sanction of her extreme need to consume and be consumed. Framing the four-sided sexual problem is the final pastoral landscape, fitting the predicament: the mountains of a Swiss ski resort in deathly frost and devastating whiteness. Here Crich dies, frozen at the bottom of a ravine. Subsequently Ursula comes to a curious mythic recognition of the ponderous animality that lies beneath Birkin's civilized self-delusion. Beside her as he drives the car, he grows stiff and monumental, "like an Egyptian Pharaoh," conveying both a real and an eternally unreal sense of animal potency. Here the reality would seem to be just as delusive as the unreality, since both depend upon something secret, insulated, and wishfully self-protective. This vitality which inexhaustibly feeds on itself is perhaps a terrible protraction of ingrown virginity. Ursula's realization, at any rate, deepens the desolate inconclusiveness of the main problem at the end.

The novel, though hovering on the borders of the ludicrous, is unmistakably, often ruthlessly, critical of its own characters. It is an attack upon men and women in whom the obstacles to freedom are shown to be sexual rather than social ones. Through his characters Lawrence is urging a more realistic attitude toward the problems of sexuality; but he also wishes to relate these problems to the natural, compelling forces of environment which men, as uniquely social creatures, fatally misuse.

Such pastoral configurations, with their criticism of manners and morals, are also strongly delineated in the didactic, heroless novels of Forster and in the many islanded predicaments of heroes in Conrad's novels. The appeal of pastoral to the Romantic temperament, shown by these novelists in different ways, is linked to a pervasive need to reconstruct society according to the urgencies of the individual soul. In this, Shelley the Platonist was at one with Shelley the social revolutionist; Wordsworth the pantheist, with Wordsworth the benevolent humanitarian. The pastoralists say that there is a paradise buried in each man's heart, a personal myth or an image in memory, which will lead him to rediscover his true relationship with nature and with other men. The poet's job is to present the vision of this harmony in practicable terms. In this way the poet legislates for his age. In this way, too, his poems—the reassertions of lost archetypes of experience—regain the world of beauty, goodness, and truth, of friendship, love, and magnanimity—those lost images of a free community among men. Where the world is no longer beset by a mechanistic determinism in nature or by factitious hierarchies and dualities, the ideal may indeed become real and one may approach a harmony with the seasons and with one's destiny, as the earliest believers in myth presumably did.

4. *The Real and the Ideal Reconciled*

What is the relation between the ideal and the symbolic types? If one takes the ideal to be the proposed norm in all types of symbolic fiction, it obviously suggests a way of converting an *as-if* world into an *as-is* world, and of measuring one against the other. To this extent the ideal, whether expressed or implied, may be the same in each symbolic type. The difference in how it is managed points to the difference between the types and to the conceptual nature of the ideal itself—universally assumed to be remote from possibility, though in different degrees desirable.

The need to go back, as in pastoral, to a state of innocence, equality, or perfection may be very differently viewed by different persons and groups. Some may deny it vehemently out of the fear of having to give up grappling with the "real" issues of a competitive life. Some may eschew it with relative equanimity while endeavoring to work somewhat more in the "present surroundings" toward a realistically better future. Others may look unrealistically toward the future—toward the surprise around the corner or the bargain of a life after death—as a way also of looking back. For many the pastoral ideal may be acceptable only embarrassedly, in paradoxical, effete, or otherwise limited terms—as, say, a joke which temporarily assuages or covers hostility. The same tension, rising out of the ambivalent attitude, finds expression in pastoral through the ironies and paradoxes of the *as-if* world beguilingly presented in the image of the world *as-is*. The more elaborate the documentation, the more covert does the ruse become, and the closer does it verge on satire.

Satire may obscure the ideal by seeming to approach it in the reverse—through a criticism of the minute particulars of the here-and-now. Behind a rich naturalistic veneer satire pretends to represent contemporary life or to render the possible results of contemporary evils; it assumes certain trends and events projected into the future, thus making the present seem a fool's paradise, a zany utopia. In this way the ideal is allowed to glimmer through only by implication. In a satire having many implications, like Kafka's, the criticism surpasses the social particularities and implies that the flagrant defects it depicts make the junking of the whole system desirable. Also, through meaningful distortions, as in showing that all moralism derives from physical limitations, the effect is to destroy the norms upon which false opinions and judgments are built. Satire tells us what Bernard Shaw's physician told him about his unusually normal eyesight: so few are so blessed that the norm becomes the exception. Satire also tells us what the psychologists often point out: that one's perception of objects depends in part upon one's psychic orientation. We readily see or notice what we wish to; and for those who pretend they see more, its advice seems to coincide with the disturbing scientific discovery that normal vision comprises only an infinitesimal degree of the whole range of the spectrum.

What if one were to take a given ideal or an absolutist ethic as entirely practicable? The answer is of course contained in Dante's exploration of "the state of souls after death," Spenser's virtue-ridden knights, *Don Quixote, The Confidence Man,* Bunyan's expeditionary account of a Christian soul's "election," Dostoevski's portrait of Mishkin the divine fool, and so on. In each instance, it is not the ideal or its practicability which is determining for us; it is the glow of an otherworldliness, the proof of other possibilities of existence beyond our knowable world. We suspend belief in witnessing another world bound by its own necessities, and layered with the purpose, irony, paradox, wisdom, justice, and truth which the fiction has realized. In this effect, which is one of making the marvelous conceivable, the ideals in all symbolic types are similar; it is in the treatment and localization of the ideal that the types differ.

And so the epic tells us that heroes are possible and also semi-divine, and that history is really the life stories of heroes—gods in human form. It thus establishes the historical-mythical prototypes of heroism in which the ideal is wedded to the action. The basic aim of epic is social and religious: to commemorate the virtues of honor and courage which have bound men together in the past, and to lay down such patterns of behavior for all men thereafter. When the terms of epical heroism are mocked or transformed according to other ethical ideas, the result is satire or pastoral, or both. When they are further rationalized and systematically redirected (as by Christian analogy, which lays stress on the individual as a type of everyman who may reach godliness), the result is allegory. Hence the ascendant or dominant temperament of a period eschews one and prefers another type of symbolic expression, depending upon how closely that type identifies its problems. To this extent the problems, like the ideals, may be similar from one age to another; the particular symbolic type chosen to express them reveals how they can best be rephrased.

There is something further to be said about the functions of myth in these connections. If it is true that literature constantly profits from the insights of philosophic systems while dispensing with their rationalistic prejudices, it seems even truer that literature dramatizes and remakes certain myths so memorably that even antagonistic philosophers are impelled subsequently to adapt the remade myths in their systems. The relationship of any literary art to myth is essentially a matter of re-establishing vital links with a personal and a cultural past. But the nature of this past and of the broken links engrosses the social researcher as well as the artist. During the last century and a half, the main effort of humane studies has gone into a delineation of the ideals through which different cultures express their will to survive, especially as seen through the actual historical conditions which often bring these cultures into conflict with individuals and groups that try to make the ideals explicit and meaningful. Such studies coincide with the renewed interest in myth among the Romantics, and with the open and implicit criticisms of society which that interest promoted. The current anthropological view that myth is a necessary function of social life suggests something about the origin of the ideal in symbolic fictions. It also tells us how the myth and the ideal each in its way sustains its appeal as an answer to man's fundamental hopes and fears.

Among many recent commentaries on the subject, Ernst Cassirer's is notably acute. The origins of myth, he tells us, are not exclusively intellectual or emotional; they are both. More specifically, myth is the *expression* of emotion—not the emotion itself but its projection and transformation into an image. The dimness and subjectivity of feeling thereby undergoes a vital change: in assuming an expressive form, it defines itself as an active process. Mythical imagination does not deal with personal confession but with the experience, the violent hopes and fears of a social group. It objectifies man's social condition by means of an imaginative art. And although myth did not pretend to deal rationally with the problem of death, which concerned the philsophers later, it alone could raise and solve the problem in an objective language that satisfied the primitive mind.[9]

In essence, these observations enjoin us to regard myth—the buried domain of feeling and expression—as a social phenomenon of primitive society that endures through the symbolic orientations of the ideal in art. To this one might add that the buried past, where men's hopes and fears are first formed, is an aspect of the individual's affective life which constantly seeks resolution in rational or intellectual terms. It creates the need to objectify social experience, and results in the symbolic shaping of myth. Both myth and symbolic fictions rise from the same source and from the same need to give transcendent expression to these problems we call social and metaphysical. The implication is that there are no conclusive answers to questions concerning death, the facts of social experience, and the personal and cultural past. This becomes evident in the continually pressing need for answers, shown by the constant rephrasing and reassertion of these questions in art.

Perhaps a final example will suffice to clarify the relationship between myth and symbolic art.

In the hero's ordeal (his solitary wanderings, his initiation into the unknown, his recognition of mission, and his return to society) there exist all the hopes for integration and all the affirmations in terms of known experience whereby societies express their will to survive. If renewal through love and death is a cliché in Romantic literature and Freudian psychology alike, the notion expresses not simply a fierce biological assertion against fate but rather a truth understood and enacted in social myths to explain the communion of men and the meaning of individual experience. Thus the change by initiation which the child undergoes at puberty, from a state of natural being to a state of adult responsibility, obviously corresponds to the moral and psychological appropriation of a new life abounding with certain integrative powers impossible to know in a former condition of "innocence." The initiation symbolizes a dying and a rebirth, a sleep and a new awakening, analogous with the cyclic forces at work in nature. In regaining selfhood, one gains or is integrated with the universe. Symbolic rites prefigure the means by which a human being comes to realization as a man, and incidentally confirm the order of society which has made this realization possible. The rites dramatize the triumph of the higher animal among his fellows, verifying the social law by which men seek to control the complex physical and psychological dangers confronting human life. One comes to see that in the territory of the myth there is a common meeting ground for Plato's Ideas, Aristotle's Causes, Kant's Categories, Freud's Id-Ego-Superego, and Jung's Archetypes. All appear to be symbolic formulations of the same mythical body which has been variously incorporated into epic, allegory, satire, and pastoral.

The clearest fact about these symbolic types is their adaptation of myths in new forms of literary art. In fiction and drama since the Renaissance there is a ceaseless assault upon intellectual pride and the old Christian and Classical images of a lost paradise. The basic view is Protestant, and culminates in the Romantic apotheosis of supermen of power and love. It is marked by a continual exploration of rationality and sexuality, embarking from the shores of reason toward a great irrational sea—as in *The Tempest,* in Swift, and in Kafka. In the act of creation—the imaginative process at work upon myths—the symbolic types take on a new life; they accept the invitation of myths to rediscover old ways of feeling and belief, the ever-new sense of the body of the world discoverable in a single individual body, in a single human experience.

A brief consideration of Joyce's typical treatment of character in the light of Spenser's typical characterizations will illustrate these general observations.

In *The Faerie Queene* the world is presented morally, as an emanation of inner experience. There the virtues and vices exist as personified motivations to action in the guise of fictional characters. Some vices, like Archimago and Duessa, are realized as persons, while those like Mammon or Despair need to wear only the obvious clothing of the psychic forces which Spenser intends them briefly to represent. But the well-drawn figures of Britomart (Chastity) and Arthur (Magnificence) surge across the border of abstraction and become vivid, dramatically incarnated personalities. In this area, where the abstract merges with the real, Joyce, working from the opposite direction—from the naturalistic to the symbolic—meets Spenser. When one considers *A Portrait of the Artist as a Young Man* and *Finnegans Wake* as extensions at the beginning and the end, respectively, of the myth-made fabric of *Ulysses,* one sees how the realistic personalities of Stephen, the Blooms, and others merge with, or are submerged in, the vast chaos of Dublin; and further, in Earwicker's dream, how they become anonymous forces with multiple names that correspond to the gigantic all-time, all-place workings in the brain of one all-man.

In *Ulysses,* where Joyce models his characters on Homer's, the transformation from naturalistic identity to symbol apparently reverses the process of characterization in *The Faerie Queene.* Stephen becomes another Telemachus looking for his spiritual father, and Leopold Bloom, another Ulysses looking for his spiritual son. Molly Bloom becomes half a waiting Penelope and half a goddess of fertility identified with a primitive Gea, mother Earth. At the same time, Stephen is the young artist-intellectual roaming Dublin's streets on a particular day, and Leopold Bloom is very much the obscure Jewish advertising agent ineffectually trespassing on his fellow citizens in the usual rounds of his daily business. Similarly, Molly Bloom is his adulterous semi-professional singer wife waiting at home for the assignation with her manager. But what happens is that they all slowly cease to exist as free-willed actors in a naturalistic setting—according to the norms of realistic fiction. They appear to have relinquished their wills to the author, who has made them specimens of unending strands of consciousness, minutely observed representatives of vast stores of psychic energy. Yet their symbolic lives are not less intense than their naturalistic lives. It is simply that the usually unexplored parts of the consciousness, their submerged being, has become the focus of characterization. As readers we seem to stand on the threshold of consciousness, momentarily looking down toward the bottomless depths where the individual dissolves into the mythical. From such a view their lives seem infinitely extensible, and also infinitely more chaotic than the symbolic role designated for them by the superimposed mythology or by their naturalistic Dublin setting. This process of alternately diffusing and condensing personality does not apply to minor characters like the two barmaids (Sirens), Gerty MacDowell (Nausicaa), and Bella Cohen (Circe). For they are only nominal symbols and nominal personalities, aborted by-products of the central action, hardly intelligible as characters except as they briefly enter the action of the story and appear in the same episodic chronology in *Ulysses* as do their counterparts in the *Odyssey*. The prefiguration in Homer barely tells us what they are as symbols in a submerged naturalistic setting. Yet they are morally and dramatically as crucial to Joyce's Odyssey as, say, Pyrochles and Cymochles or the Lady Phaedria are to Guyon's adventures in Book Two of *The Faerie Queene*. For they exist both as obstacles and temptations—the wedged-in shapes of appetite and yearning distracting the main characters' progress —and as projections of Bloom's and Dedalus' consciousnesses, which have begun to take in the whole mythical existence of chaotic Dublin. Where Spenser's final vision of fancy-ridden fairyland—comprising both Elizabethan England and the arena of moral consciousness—presents Nature triumphing over the forces of Mutability, Joyce's final vision in *Finnegans Wake* is significantly different. For there the Word of the writer appears throughout as creative principle and as representational instrument. In this way it overrides, without needing to resolve, the moral dilemma into which Dedalus and Bloom have faded with their existential problems, becoming part of a gigantic, unbroken, cyclic symbolism which, like a perpetual-motion machine, provides its own energy in a never-ending process of coming into being.

Each symbolic type admits a reconciliation of the ideal with the real world if the reader implicitly accepts the fiction's commitment to the values of the hypothetical world the writer has constructed and regained from time. We learn this from the allegorical designs in widely different examples; we learn that the coalescence of moral aim and esthetic fulfillment results from a distinctive way of viewing a mythic subject matter. The figurative representation in a concrete particular becomes the poetic integer—the metaphor in action, the image of what is possible. This happens in a fictional context only when the theme is made valid, not as an article of unquestioning faith but, as the old anagoge was, the goal in proof of which the action finally tends. And this is why in all symbolic fictions we return at the end to the comprehensive statement of the theme—Dante's "state of souls after death"; Melville's "overwhelming idea of the whale"; Spenser's love visions in the framework of mutability. We return, in other words, to the literal level of narrative in which is impacted the fundamental meanings and unity of the whole work. The conceivable and practicable ideal is the forge upon which the method is hammered out and perfected; without it the method, all of symbolic art itself, would not exist and would have no reason for existing.

In Sum

THE QUESTIONS that have persistently been asked about allegory may be reduced to this: Is it a stuffing made to fill out a preconceived structure or theory that opposes a realistic—objective, pragmatic, experiential—view of life, and so in effect, to paraphrase Henry James, is responsible for the world's most forcible-feeble sort of writing? The answer opens on a bewildering multitude of problems related to the uses of symbolism in literature. We can only recapitulate the conclusions to which the investigation of a few of these problems has led.

In one of its aspects allegory is a rhetorical instrument used by strategists of all sorts in their struggle to gain power or to maintain a system of beliefs. (Such usage and the motives lurking behind it have recently had the close study of critics as part of the semantic problem of symbolic action.) In addition to serving the expression of ideological aims, allegory is a fundamental device of hypothetical construction. In this broad way allegory is part of the creative process, observable in all literature generally, where the formulation of vital beliefs seems essential to maximum expressiveness.

The literary allegory does not oppose a realistic account of the universe. Its very power lies in its giving proof to the physical and ethical realities of life objectively conceived. This it does typically in the narrative course by moving progressively backward, forward, and upward on a three-dimensional continuum. Thus the progression of an allegory is spiral—virtually

179

simultaneous in all three directions: backward to the thing represented (the story, the literal depiction of reality), which is itself symbolic, pregnant with signification, and forward and upward to the consummation of its meaning in the whole work. The symbolic nature of the literal dimension evokes in the reader the recognition that his own experience parallels the expanding implications of the symbolic material in the narrative. The resolution of the symbol in the transumptive meaning of the whole work confirms the reader's understanding of his own experience by showing how its gradually perceived potentialities are eventually fulfilled.

As a conceptual instrument allegory makes possible a cosmic view of the intrinsic relationships of all objects and beings, each of which, by attribute or action, discloses in respect to itself the typical likeness and unlikeness in every other object and being. Thus as concept allegory serves to define or devise states of separateness and togetherness, oppositions and unities. But in the practical completion of its design, the allegorical work dispenses with the concept of allegory, as something preconceived, in order to achieve the fullest fictional manifestation of life. Allegory, which is symbolic in method, is realistic in aim and in the content of its perception.

Just as the concept of allegory, when taken prescriptively, leads to a limited personification allegory, so only the programmatic brand of realism is antagonistic to allegory. The products of programmatic realism and prescriptive allegory lack a foothold in reality; both deny the representative, confuse the universal with the particular, and neglect the moral qualifications that make experience meaningful. An imaginative poverty of this sort pervades late nineteenth-century naturalism, the slice-of-life sort of realism. Following almost verbatim Claude Bernard's medical treatise, Zola in *The Experimental Novel* adduces the same mechanistic determinism for art and life—a simplified heredity-environment formula—that Bernard found operating in natural processes and organisms. It is true that Zola's theory has a representative aim and implementation in

fiction. But it goes wrong on two accounts: first, in simply serving a laboratory theory that "explains" life before the writer has
fictionalized it; secondly, because the method of representation,
endlessly concerned with "proving instances," results in the
defect of overparticularization. One encounters the opposite
extreme—misrepresentation by overuniversalizing—among the
French symbolists. By emphasizing esthetic or sensory effects
to the exclusion of objective reality, they dispense with the
particularities upon which a vital art depends. The symbol becomes an arbitrary fixation of the artist's, an esthetic com-
forter to warm his metaphysics. In following literally a wholly
subjective or deterministic theory about life and art, French
symbolism and Zola's naturalism impoverish the nature of experience in art. Neither has a truly objective or truly symbolic
foothold in reality.

The Romantic esthetic, adapted from the criticism of Kant,
Vico, and Lessing, is largely responsible for the prejudice
against allegory in our time, and for destroying the ontologi-
cal basis of symbolism so that it becomes a personal fetish of
the artist's. Inheriting the Protestant idea of individual self-determination, and fortified by a sense of life's ambiguities and
paradoxes, the Romantic esthetic broke off the chain relating
man to other creatures and to the inanimate world. It jetti-
soned not only the traditional symbolism of Christian analogy
but also the cosmology of the natural sciences along with its
humanitarian ideals and its belief in the possibility of controlling nature unaided by providence. In losing its objective character, the symbol became a simulacrum, a disembodied form
in which ideas or feelings were arbitrarily substituted for real
events, persons, and things. The symbolism of the French
symbolists became another version of the reality-drained personification allegory of the Middle Ages. The current prejudice
against literary allegory which derives from this source is really
an expression of dissatisfaction with the concept of allegory,
and with the idea that art—an autonomous product of the
imagination, a thing-in-itself—has any business with beliefs or

purposes. These notions are not, of course, attributable to the forerunners of the Romantic esthetic; indeed, the philosophic tenets of Lessing, Vico, and Kant are often directly opposed to them.

We have considered the questions of religious and philosophic belief aroused by this reactionary esthetics as intrinsic to the problem of relating method and ideal in allegorical fiction. A literary allegory that converts problematic issues of experience into the metaphors of its own organic design does not depend upon moralistic icons or professions of faith in a specific religion. Moreover, religious belief as represented by theological systems is simply one form in which a belief in man's destiny has been expressed. Art, philosophy, psychology, and science are other forms. In this light, the Christian codification of the concept of fourfold meaning appears neither unique in aim nor restrictive of the allegorical process in literature. It marks an ideological phase in the development of the concept of allegory, occurring as the result of one adaptation from a regnant system of beliefs. Because of Dante's influence, the medieval conception has become the fount of our understanding, but also of our misunderstanding, of literary allegory. Critical reconsiderations of the analogical formula in a contemporary context have been advanced by Kenneth Burke in his work on motives, by Northrop Frye in his critical studies of Blake and of centripetal meaning, and by Erich Auerbach in his account of the development of realism in literature. And as the findings of such critics emerge there are indications that contemporary ideals offer the same high possibilities of literary embodiment as did the medieval Christian ideals, for integrating individual and cultural consciousness.

We have come round at the end to where we began—to the view that current literary symbology, so much indulged in and taking so many different terminological byways, is pursuing neither a newfangled nor an anachronistic hare. Impelled by a new urgency, this pursuit expresses an age-old necessity of the spirit to discern its image in the unity of some created invention where all of life's teeming multiplicities flash by—now in full sight, now in shadow, and now wrapped in life's own darkness. As such, the search for symbolic meaning is an essential part of the effort to name and renew a full awareness of reality in contemporary terms.

It may be that this whole appraisal of allegory will be reduced by some, in Shakespeare's words, to "brains beguil'd,/ Which, labouring for invention, bear amiss/The second burden of a former child." But those who see it in this way will only see what allegory must always have seemed to them originally— an unfortunate still-birth. To this view of the subject one is inclined to reply that the sun can be looked at steadily only through smoked glass. As Wallace Stevens has remarked, "how clean the sun when seen in its idea." And so the idea of allegory may only be—to invoke Stevens again—a "name for something that never could be named" and actually should "bear no name" other than "inconceivable idea," existing "in the difficulty of what it is to be."

Notes

I. Foreground

1. For constructive criticisms of this view, see George Whalley, "A Note on Allegory," *Poetic Process* (1953), pp. 190–192, and Northrop Frye, *Anatomy of Criticism* (1957), pp. 89–91.

2. In descent from Kant's critical philosophy such a view emphasizes the artist's quest for freedom as the chief determinant of the creative process. In *The Psychology of Art* (trans. Stuart Gilbert, 1953) André Malraux shows that the quest for freedom appears as indelibly in retrospect as "a star whose light still reaches us, though it has ceased to exist." Cutting through the controversy in esthetics over value and function, Malraux insists on the primary point of the work's contemporaneity as perceived by the spectator of whatever age. (Although he is concerned with pictorial art, his theory holds for literary art as well.) He argues that the effort to restore the feeling of the work's own time often succeeds only in returning it to the sacrosanct precincts for which it served a simple unambiguous function or value. In this light the work becomes only a fragment, "always deprived of something, if only of the setting of its age." On the other hand, the individual genius who fully achieves his quest for freedom is likely to seem a destroyer, someone who "breaks forth from the conventional in the same way as from the crude or inchoate: by destroying it, so as to establish the significance of that which it prefigures."

A similar point is eloquently made by Northrop Frye in "Levels of Meaning in Literature" (*The Kenyon Review*, Spring 1950):

> One of the first laws of literature is that morally the lion lies down with the lamb. Bunyan and Rochester, Jane Austen and Huysmans, Shakespeare's sublimity and Shakespeare's obscenity, all belong together. Morality, like truth, is not *within* literature at all, and to derive moral values from it we must again approach it from outside. So far from being "moral" in any direct sense, the moral value of art seems actually to have something to do with the breaking down of customary moral reactions. This arises from the very nature of art as hypothetical. Morality

185

is constantly tending to incorporate itself in a series of implied or expressed affirmations. But as soon as morality has decided one thing, the poet is apt to hypothesize another; and, as with truth, the affirmation limits, and the hypothesis seems to have something to do with emancipation or deliverance from the affirmation even if we believe the affirmation to be true or good.

3. It may be noted that the same analogy appears, among other places, in St. Matthew and 1 Corinthians. These are the relevant parts of the speech in Shakespeare:

> There was a time when all the body's members
> Revell'd against the belly; thus accus'd it:
> That only like a gulf it did remain
> I' the midst o' the body, idle and unactive,
> Still cupboarding the viand, never bearing
> Like labour with the rest, where the other instruments
> Did see and hear, devise, instruct, walk, feel,
> And, mutually participate, did minister
> Unto the appetite and affection common
> Of the whole body. The belly answer'd,—
> . . . "True is it, my incorporate friends," quoth he,
> "That I receive the general food at first,
> Which you do live upon; and fit it is;
> Because I am the store-house and the shop
> Of the whole body: but, if you do remember,
> I send it through the rivers of your blood,
> Even to the court, the heart, to the seat o' the brain;
> The strongest nerves and small inferior veins
> From me receive that natural competency
> Whereby they live. And though that all at once,
> You, my good friends," —this says the belly, mark me,
> . . . "Though all at once cannot
> See what I do deliver out to each,
> Yet I can make my audit up, that all
> From me do back receive the flour of all,
> And leave me but the bran." What say you to 't?
> . . . The senators of Rome are this good belly,
> And you the mutinous members; for, examine
> Their counsels and their cares, digest things rightly

Touching the weal o' the common, you shall find
No public benefit which you receive
But it proceeds or comes from them to you,
And no way from yourselves. What do you think,
You, the great toe of this assembly?
    (I, i: 101–110; 136–147; 148–152; 154–161)

II. Conception

In addition to the works cited below, other historical and philo-
sophical commentaries that have served as general references in
this chapter are: Wilhelm Windelband, *A History of Philosophy*,
Vols. 1 and 2 (trans. James H. Tufts, 1901); Ernst Cassirer, *An
Essay on Man* (1944); Denis de Rougemont, *Love in the Western
World* (1956); and C. S. Lewis, *The Allegory of Love* (1936).

1. See Numa Denis Fustel de Coulanges, *The Ancient City* (trans.
W. Small, 1874).

2. See R. R. Marett, *Sacraments of the Simple Folk* (1933).

3. The etymology of *myth* and *mystery* and the curious modifica-
tions which the words have undergone are vividly surveyed by
Erich Kahler in "The Persistence of Myth," *Chimera*, Spring 1946:

> The Greek word *mythos*, most etymologists believe, goes
> back to *mü, mu*, which imitates an elementary sound such as
> the lowing of cattle, the growl of beasts or of thunder, and
> originally meant inarticulate sounding of all kinds: bellowing,
> booming, roaring (Lat. *mugire*, Fr. *mugir*), murmuring, hum-
> ming, rumbling, groaning, muttering, or, in humans, non-verbal
> utterance with closed lips—and, by derivation, the closing
> of the mouth; *mut*eness (Lat. *mut*us). From the same root
> comes the Greek verb *müein, myein*, to close up, to close the
> eyes, from which derive *mystery* and *mystic*, the secret rites
> and teaching. Myth and mystery, then, are connected in their
> origin.
>
> By the linguistic process that so often turns a word into its
> opposite—as in the case of the Latin *muttire*, to mutter, and

mutus, mute, becoming the French *mot,* word—the Greek *mu,* signifying inarticulate voicing with closed mouth, evolved into *mythos,* word.

And yet the meaning of the root sound carried over into the specialized meaning the Greeks ultimately attached to *mythos.* The poets and writers of early periods used *mythos* indiscriminately in the sense of *word* (Homer, for instance, in contraposition to *ergon,* deed); they scarcely distinguished it from other Greek terms for *word: epos* and *logos.* But gradually the uses become specific: *mythos* becomes the word as the most ancient, the most original account of the origins of the world, in divine revelation or sacred tradition, of gods and demi-gods and the genesis of the cosmos, cosmogony; and it comes to be sharply contrasted with *epos,* the word as human narration, and— from the Sophists on—with *logos,* the word as rational construction.

4. The most familiar example of this phenomenon is the Bible; according to the Christian view, the Old Testament becomes a figure for the New, and one is asked to read the New Testament as a "fulfillment" of the Old.

5. Gilbert Murray, *The Rise of the Greek Epic* (1907), pp. 158–159.

6. The phrase "the work itself" drags up tricky questions often pondered by critics. When and to whom is the work a thing in itself? Before the commentators have had their chance at it? To that implausible reader who accepts it for itself alone and not for any potentially extricable body of meaning in it? Or to the writer, the only begetter, who unlike God could not have had "everything in mind" when he wrote it but seems to have written it as if he did? Although endlessly provocative for theory-making, these questions are probably insoluble.

One may add one's own conjectures, however. First, as with man's view of nature and his surroundings, the work itself is always to some extent just what a reader understands it to be, what he takes it for. Secondly, the work in one age may lend itself to such a specialized kind of interpretation that it can no longer be seen in anything like the original spirit in which it was written, when it offered "something to everybody." Thirdly, the very accumulation and encrustation of meanings around the work dissuade one from seeing it in its original state, whatever that may have been, just as in its working out, the book twists and turns developmentally in response to the maker's resources, to all the conscious and unconscious forces influencing him at the time of composition. Finally, the work-in-itself will seem alive as long as it retains a magical, mana-like hold on its readers.

Like a tree, which is constantly affected by its surroundings, it is always gradually dying. Yet even when "dead," it may still be beautiful, much as the *Iliad* and the *Odyssey*, which, although no longer believed in as *myth*, are still read as literature.

7. The results of the differences between historicist and allegorist over the nature of the gods are more pronounced in tragic drama. In their adaptations from the popular religious mythology the Greek dramatists showed how a powerful art could be created out of a symbolism and a faith which had already been discredited. This is noted by Francis Fergusson in *The Idea of a Theater* (1949); he writes with regard to Sophocles, who "would not, for his purpose, have had to ask himself whether the myth of Oedipus conveyed any historical facts. He would not have had to believe that the performance of *Oedipus*, or even the festival of Dionysos itself, would assure the Athenians a good crop of children and olives. On the contrary, he must have felt that the tragic rhythm of action which he discerned in the myth, which he felt as underlying the forms of the ritual, and which he realized in so many ways in his play, was a deeper version of human life than any particular manifestation of it, or any conceptual understanding of it, whether scientific and rationalistic, or theological; yet potentially including them all." (p. 47)

The implication is not that a cultural lag existed in drama but that a highly individual artistic consciousness had asserted itself. Unlike Aristophanes, the tragic dramatists were not satirizing the popular religion. They were resurrecting its affective appeal, the mythopoeic imagination which had originally invested it, and refashioning the myth in a new form. The mystery that had animated the old myth, and had begun to lapse under the rationalistic interpretation, was thus revitalized. The form had changed—it was now drama, not ritual or history or epic poetry—and the new enactment incorporated the rationalistic disbelief within the traditional narrative frame of the myth.

On the evidence of such embodiments of experience, Aristotle was enabled to distinguish the uses of history and art, and to create a theory of esthetics. Myth from different contexts is similarly renewed in Dante, Spenser, the Elizabethan and Classical French drama, and in certain Romantic and symbolic novels. In each instance the reinspirited myth provides a new version of the adaptive procedures typical of literary allegory.

8. Ideally the "figure" and its "fulfillment" at the heart of Christian analogy should present, according to the early theologians, a universal picture of history and nature from the beginnings of time. Starting with the early Church fathers, the analogical tradition had hammered this ideal into a rigid code and a polemical instrument. By the thirteenth century the ideal had become a battered rationale subserving political and ecclesiastic programs, and grown into one type of sin which Dante portrayed in the *Commedia*. Erich Auerbach's admirable account of the poem in *Mimesis* (trans. Willard R. Trask, 1953) selects as the most determining factor in Dante's achievement his unified conception of time from "the figural point of view." This view, he writes, "enables us to understand that the beyond is eternal and yet phenomenal; that it is changeless and of all time and yet full of history. It also enables us to show in what way this realism in the beyond is distinguished from every type of purely earthly realism. In the beyond man is no longer involved in any earthly representation of human events. Rather, he is involved in an eternal situation which is the sum and the result of all his actions and which at the same time tells him what were the decisive aspects of his life and his character. Thus his memory is led along a path which, though for the inhabitants of Hell it is dreary and barren, is yet always the right path, the path which reveals what was decisive in the individual's life. In this condition the dead present themselves to the living Dante. The suspense inherent in the yet unrevealed future—an essential element in all earthly concerns and their artistic imitation, especially of a dramatic, serious and problematic kind—has ceased. In the Comedy only Dante can feel this suspense. The many played-out dramas are combined in one great play, involving his own fate and that of all mankind; they are exempla of the winning or losing of eternal bliss. But passions, torments, and joys have survived; they find expression in the situations, gestures, and utterances of the dead.

With Dante as spectator, all the dramas are played over again in tremendously concentrated form. . . . And in them, seemingly scattered and fragmented, yet actually always as parts within a general plan, the history of Florence, of Italy, of the world, unfolds. Suspense and development, the distinguishing characteristics of earthly phenomena, are no more. Yet the waves of history do reach the shores of the world beyond; partly as memories of the earthly past; partly as interest in the earthly present; partly as concern for the earthly future; in all cases as a temporality figurally preserved in timeless eternity. Each of the dead interprets his condition in the beyond as the last act, forever being played out, of his earthly drama." (pp. 197–198)

In the *Commedia,* as Auerbach concludes, Dante bursts the abstraction-making mechanism, "the figural-Christian view"; ". . . the image of man eclipses the image of God," and in its fulfillment, the figure emerges and takes on an independent reality. We see a similar phenomenon unfolding in the works of later allegorists— Spenser, Hawthorne, Melville, Kafka—when their fictional adaptations of familiar symbolic schema transcend these conceptions in the literary realization.

9. The new literary ideal of courtly love has its source in Christian analogy, or the tradition of insight symbolism, as H. Flanders Dunbar calls it in *Symbolism and Medieval Thought* (1929):

> Among those in sympathy with the development of the tradition which Dante used, no question of "either-or" could arise in connection with symbolic levels of meaning. Beatrice is not *either* a real girl *or* a symbol of love, but a real girl *and* a symbol of love *and* of the Holy Spirit *and* of the Divine Sun. . . . With insight symbol it is not a matter of saying one thing and meaning another, as in cryptograms and secret codes. "Either-or" comes more easily to the adolescent mind than "both-and" but "both-and" states the truth of traditional insight symbolism. (pp. 490, 493)

In distinguishing between Dante's use of the insight symbol and the conventional medieval treatment of personification allegory, the statement points to the strength of the foundation upon which he was building the new romantic ideal. Dante's treatment of it in the

Commedia may partially account for the richness and force of the ideal, even after it deserted the Christian figural view, in its later literary developments.

10. In *The Philosophy of Analogy and Symbolism* (1947), S. T. Cargill writes,

> One of the chief points of controversy between the religions of the West and those of the East is that the Christian peoples of the former worship the Third Logos as a Masculine Holy Ghost and the non-Christian peoples of the latter worship the Third Logos as a Feminine Holy Ghost. The teaching of the Gnostics which reconciled the two was rejected by the Episcopacy when the Creeds were drawn up. . . . (p. 94)

11. This is true of the *Roman* no less than of Racine's drama, of *Madame Bovary*, and of Proust's masterwork. One thinks of Proust particularly in reading A. B. Taylor's account of Jean de Meun's contribution to the *Roman*:

> The chief feature of his work is a formal, conventional and systematic analysis of love; every emotion and sentiment of the lovers of both sexes is fully analysed, and the courtly spirit enhanced by a detailed description of armour and dresses, of tournaments and adventures, and of the scenes where the main incidents occur. *Introduction to Medieval Romance* (1930), p. 64.

To apply this observation to *Remembrance of Things Past,* one has only to substitute "aristocratic" or "nouveau riche" for "courtly," "social masks" for "armour," and "salons and parties" or "verbal jousts" for "tournaments"—though in this way one would be accounting only for the surface layer of an essentially profound exploration of the human psyche. The *Roman* is a story—and here Racine's *Bérénice* might also be included—in which, as Taylor concludes,

> the heroine falls in love rather with the idea of love than with a man whose merit would be likely to attract enduring esteem. And the interest of such stories lies not in the depth or strength

of emotions portrayed, but in the accurate reflection of life and the minute analysis of the lovers' sentiments. (p. 240)

12. Erich Fromm in *The Forgotten Language* (1951) discusses this connection between Greek drama and the "motherright" theory.

13. *Miscellaneous Criticism,* ed. T. M. Raysor (1936), p. 30.

14. *Ibid.*

15. *Lectures on Shakespeare and Milton,* IX.

16. *Biographia Literaria,* XIII.

17. The term symbolist-in-retreat applies to the post-Coleridgean writer caught between a critical defense of his own art and his assault upon all types of art which seem to falsify, or to distort by simplifying, the difficult problematic character of man's destiny. The symbolist-in-retreat retreats from any view which would identify his method and ideals with a predetermined moral or esthetic schema, particularly when, as with allegory, such schemas appear to suggest his own prepossessions. But he is likewise in retreat from an irresponsible eclecticism in art, and from scientistic or psychologistic theories which make art subservient to social causes and ameliorative programs. The symbolist-in-retreat is the artist, poet, or novelist who attempts to assimilate his culture in experimental works but whose works exist outside the conventions of his time.

18. The phrase appears in Melville's letter of January 8, 1852, to Sophia Hawthorne. The relevant passage is worth recalling:

But then, since you, with your spiritualizing nature, see more things than other people, and by the same process, refine all you see, so that they are not the same things that other people see, but things which while you think you but humbly discover them, you do in fact create for yourself—therefore, upon the whole I do not so much marvel at your expressions concerning Moby Dick. At any rate, your allusion for example to the "spirit Spout" first showed to me that there was a subtile significance in that thing—but I did not, in that case, *mean* it. I had some vague idea while writing it, that the book was susceptible of an allegoric construction, & also that *parts* of it were—but the specialty of many of the particular subordinate

allegories, were first revealed to me, after reading Mr. Hawthorne's letter, which, without citing any particular examples,
yet intimated the part-&-parcel allegoricalness of the whole.

Melville's reply seems more than a polite acknowledgment of
Mrs. Hawthorne's ingenious reading and praise of the novel. It is
quite probable that Melville, at the instigation of the Hawthornes,
was coming around to a more receptive opinion of allegory and its
possibilities as a literary instrument. As F. O. Matthiessen points
out in *American Renaissance* (1941), the friendship and inter-
change between Hawthorne and Melville occurred when both men
were at the peak of their creative powers. It is also notable, as
Matthiessen suggests, that following the Hawthorne-Melville correspondence about *Moby Dick*, Melville wrote *Pierre*, in which he
uses the term allegory as a synonym for profundity, and that the
novel contains several striking allegorical insets, like the one in
the chapter on the Enceladus myth, in addition to frequent allusions
to Dante and Bunyan.

19. *Miscellaneous Criticism*, ed. T. M. Raysor (1936), p. 30.

20. E. A. Poe, "Hawthorne's Tales," from *The Shock of Recognition*,
ed. E. Wilson (1943).

21. Henry James, "Hawthorne," from *The Shock of Recognition*,
ed. E. Wilson (1943).

22. One might say of modern symbolists-in-retreat that they are
allegorists-in-retreat as well, since any quest for a new literary adaptation of a vital esthetic and ethical ideal, particularly after Kant,
seems fated to run into the opposition of a culture which no longer
actively supports a symbolic orientation in its major beliefs, but
which is otherwise momentously affected by the symbolic methods
of specialized disciplines in the natural and social sciences. Writers
who sensed the significance of such a reversed orientation turned
into satirists (e.g., Melville, Kafka, Joyce, *et al.*) in reaction to the
loss of all forms of symbolic nurture in modern society. Simultaneously they turned against the pervading flatness of a naturalistic,
stimulus-bound psychologism in fiction which really pays lip serv-
ice to legalistic morality and neglects the problematic nature of
man. Symbolists and allegorists are increasingly defensive because

they work against the cultural grain in trying to carry forward a tradition of insight based on the concept of the dignity of man— out of which modern society evolved. They know that in these attempts they must constantly envisage the possibility of a renewed fulfillment of the concept by combining the neglected ideals of the past with the emergent ideals of the present.

The current interest in "symbolic" writers like Joyce, Kafka, Faulkner, and Mann is partly explained in that they all seem to be reworking religious materials without, however, professing to believe the institutionalized morality that usually inheres in such materials. They can do this because they apparently have assimilated a vast amount of insight into man's condition from current psychological and anthropological theories, which reinforce their vision of possibility. One is tempted to say that it may no longer be the way of the allegorist to retreat into satire once the ground held by such writers has become a common heritage and a source of vitality to those whose beliefs are not distilled into mere resignation or whose convictions do not succumb to a sense of personal guilt.

23. *A Rhetoric of Motives* (1950), p. 14.

III. Construction

1. Another allegorical figuration of the life of Christ is traditionally based on Exodus, Moses being the "type" of Christ, the spiritual Israel who returns from Egypt to assault the Promised Land. "Type" is the technical word here for those Old Testament figures who are seen as prophetic foreshadowings of Christ.

2. As in a scientific experiment, which deals with empirical evidence, it is only after the hypothesis has been related to the evidence and the conclusion that the work becomes subject to criticism. But considered ideally and in process, the literal sense —like the experiment with its resultant conclusions, which are aspects of both declared and undeclared assumptions—is itself uncriticizable.

3. C. S. Sherrington, the distinguished physiologist, pictures the brain during sleep in these vivid terms:

A scheme of lines and nodal points, gathered together at one end into a great ravelled knot, the brain, and at the other trailing off to a sort of stalk, the spinal cord. Imagine activity in this shown by little points of light. Of these some stationary flash rhythmically, faster or slower. Others are travelling points, streaming in serial trains at various speeds. The rhythmic stationary lights lie at the nodes. The nodes are both goals whither converge, and junctions whence diverge, the lines of travelling lights. . . .

Suppose we choose the hour of deep sleep. Then only in some sparse and out of the way places are nodes flashing and trains of light-points running. Such places indicate local activity still in progress. . . . The great knotted head-piece of the whole sleeping system lies for the most part dark, and quite especially so the roof-brain. Occasionally at places in it lighted points flash or move but soon subside. . . .

Should we continue to watch the scheme we should observe after a time an impressive change which suddenly accrues. In the great head-end which has been mostly darkness spring up myriads of twinkling stationary lights and myriads of trains of moving lights of many different directions. It is as though activity from one of those local places which continued restless in the darkened main-mass suddenly spread far and wide and invaded all. . . . The brain is waking and with it the mind is returning. It is as if the Milky Way entered upon some cosmic dance. Swiftly the head-mass becomes an enchanted loom where millions of slashing shuttles weave a dissolving pattern, always a meaningful pattern though never an abiding one; a shifting harmony of subpatterns. . . . This means that the body is up and rises to meet its waking day. *Man on His Nature* (2d. ed., 1953), pp. 183–184.

4. Arthur Koestler, *Insight and Outlook* (1949), p. 374.

5. A familiar doctrinal version appears in 1 Corinthians 15:

Then they also which are fallen asleep in Christ are perished. But now is Christ risen from the dead, and become the first fruits of them that slept.

> For since by man came death, by man came also the resurrection of the dead.
>
> For as in Adam all die, even so in Christ shall all be made alive.

There is obviously a way in which these sentences of Paul's relate to Koestler's. Both emphasize regression as the significant condition for successful regeneration. Not without regressing to the old Adam, the overwhelming confusion of chaos, and not without succumbing in sleep to the old Adam's fleshly hopelessness, in denial of spirit, can there be the death-and-sleep defying movement upward, the regenerative shaping of consciousness and spirit toward complete integration.

6. In literary types related to allegory (pastoral, satire, epic) there is often an inverted dream induction. As in Kafka's fiction, the setting and chronology are inherently realistic rather than fantastic or patently imaginary. The dream world the reader is invited to enter, for instance, in More's *Utopia, The Tempest, Rasselas,* or *Gulliver's Travels* is a hypothetical form of the world of everyday reality. Because it draws one into a step-by-step recognition of this fact, the device suggests that the author's purpose is didactic. The inversion works somewhat like the beguiling illusion Alice accepts in stepping through the looking-glass: there the world seems to compare in most ways with the one on "the other side," except that the slight differences, when they are scrutinized, are just what make *everything* different.

7. The guiding intelligence can be evil or simply misdirective; it may function ambivalently, since it is produced by the hero's own consciousness, e.g., Faust and Mephisto, Ivan Karamazov and the devil. In *Don Juan,* Otto Rank shows that the guiding intelligence in Romantic literature is often a (living or dead) brother, friend, or father; or he is so closely related to the hero that he easily assumes all his personal traits and becomes his double, e.g., Poe's William Wilson, Dostoevski's Golyadkin, Stevenson's Jekyll-Hyde, and so forth. No small part of the Romantic's gift is his ability to hide the personification symbol of "the other self" behind separate fictional characterizations. Dickens, who learned a good deal from Bunyan and inspired Dostoevski and Kafka, often multiplied his charac-

ters in this fashion to a degree far beyond the practice of most realistic novelists. See, for example, *Bleak House, Edwin Drood, Barnaby Rudge*.

8. A crucial name, since *fidèle* (faithful) is both the standard of this ship of fools (their mounting suspicion is invariably climaxed by a fit of overtrustfulness) and an ironic synonym describing the Confidence Man's stock-in-trade.

9. The ambivalent spirit in which these maxims are presented saturates the whole novel. Through the agency of the Confidence Man in his various disguises, it attempts to show how Pauline teachings and the Beatitudes are generally perverted. The moral virtues from 1 Corinthians are pre-eminently social injunctions that readily lend themselves to the enthusiastic and optimistic pietism squeezed out of nineteenth-century American transcendentalism, whose shallowness Melville was satirizing in the novel.

Thus "Charity thinketh no evil," while suggesting the virtues of innocence and altruism, if taken superficially amounts to a denial of experience which continually proves the opposite, i.e., man's capacity for doing evil to his fellow man. "Charity suffereth long, and is kind," although implying patience and persevering kindliness, may also be seen as a preachment denying the possibility of dealing justly with different people in different situations. "Charity endureth all things" would seem to define superhuman fortitude and self-discipline; yet it may reflect intellectual blindness and the refusal or inability to recognize the opinions of others and thus to contend with them openly and honestly. "Charity believeth all things" may be a formula for unswerving faith, but it also invites overtrustfulness and gullibility, a bland self-deceptiveness that makes one unable to profit from experience. "Charity never faileth" suggests the benevolent effects of philanthropic virtue, but it must also be regarded as a self-righteous scruple which opposes the testimony of experience and thereby cruelly fails, as the novel shows, because it does not recognize the real, particular needs of individuals.

These Pauline virtues, presumably all definitive of charity, are ceaselessly questioned by Melville as the asylum of all moralistic shibboleths and unexamined premises which misrepresent the nature of man's experience in society.

10. There is a pertinent statement in *The Confidence Man* (Chapter 44) about original characters in fiction:

> . . . the original character, essentially such, is like a revolving Drummond light, raying away from itself all round it—everything is lit by it, everything starts up to it (mark how it is with Hamlet) so that, in certain minds, there follows upon the adequate conception of such a character, an effect, in its way, akin to that which in Genesis attends upon the beginning of things.

11. Joseph Campbell has summarized the narrative formula in many heroic myths by tracing its basic features in what he calls the monomyth:

> The mythological hero, setting forth from his commonday hut or castle, is lured, carried away, or else voluntarily proceeds, to the threshold of adventure. There he encounters a shadow presence that guards the passage. The hero may defeat or conciliate this power and go alive into the kingdom of the dark (brother-battle, dragon-battle; offering, charm), or be slain by the opponent and descend in death (dismemberment, crucifixion). Beyond the threshold, then, the hero journeys through a world of unfamiliar yet strangely intimate forces, some of which severely threaten him (tests), some of which give magical aid (helpers). When he arrives at the nadir of the mythological round, he undergoes a supreme ordeal and gains his reward. The triumph may be represented as the hero's sexual union with the goddess-mother of the world (sacred marriage), his own divinization (apotheosis) or again—if the powers have remained unfriendly to him—his theft of the boon he came to gain (bridge-theft, fire-theft); intrinsically it is an expansion of consciousness and therewith of being (illumination, transfiguration, freedom). The final work is that of the return. If the powers have blessed the hero, he now sets forth under their protection (emissary); if not, he flees and is pursued (transformation flight, obstacle flight). At the return threshold the transcendental powers must remain behind; the hero re-emerges from the kingdom of dread (return, resur-

rection). The boon that he brings restores the world (elixir).
The Hero with a Thousand Faces (1949), pp. 245–246.

IV. Authority

1. Spenser is also the first Englishman to make poetry out of the
fathomless tangle of medieval allegory: beast fables, homiletics, moralities, hymns, and sermon literature. And though he invents story
as well, it is not *as* story on a par with Chaucer's—the Chaucer who
is only fragmentarily an allegorical poet, but otherwise a more natural borrower from the Italian story writers than Spenser. For Spenser, like his own Dragon of Errour, must have had to ingest and
vomit out books before he could assume he had established himself
among his peers—the masters not only of his own language but of
all languages living and dead. His thoroughgoing archaism is thus
his way of linking immensely comprehensive literary aims with the
styles and subjects of his predecessors.

2. For these observations on the preface I am indebted to Jose-
phine W. Bennett's original analysis in *The Evolution of 'The Faerie
Queene'* (1942). She argues convincingly that the letter to Raleigh
represents a rationalization of a rather different scheme undertaken
earlier in a decidedly more lighthearted spirit.

3. This esthetic principle, according to which art is taken to be a
reflective force and re-embodiment of nature—and consequently,
like man, a part of nature itself—descends from Christian analogy.
Shakespeare affirms one aspect of this view in a well-known passage
of *The Winter's Tale:*

> *Perdita:* For I have heard it said
> There is an art which, in their piedness, shares
> With great creating nature.

> *Polixenes:* Say there be;
> Yet nature is made better by no mean,
> But nature makes that mean; so, o'er that art
> Which you say adds to nature is an art

That nature makes. You see, sweet maid, we marry
A gentler scion to the wildest stock,
And make conceive a bark of baser kind
By bud of nobler race. This is an art
Which does mend nature,—change it rather; but
The art itself is nature.

(IV, iv, 86–97)

4. See the analysis of this story which follows, pp. 134–37.

5. Another way of taking this documentation is to say that it is both functional in the poem and intrinsic to the poem's total conception. Such a view is adopted by Isabel E. Rathbone in *The Meaning of Spenser's Fairyland* (1937):

> Spenser's Fairyland is a land of fame, resembling the classical Elysium. The fairies are the race of gods and heroes who in their earthly lives anticipated the fame of Arthur and the future worthies who were destined to revive it. Arthur's visit to Fairyland, like the similar visits of classical epic heroes to the lower world, is preparatory to his accomplishment of his earthly mission, and *The Faerie Queene*, like *The Divine Comedy*, is a literary descendant of the Sixth Book of the *Aeneid*. (p. vii)

One may accept this explanation and still have the sense of structural defect in the burdensome presentation of the documents in II, 10 and 11, or the abruptly self-defensive tone in the proem to Book Two.

6. Shakespeare, whom Melville read avidly, seems to be dramatizing a similar conflict in Timon's gullibility and pessimism, in Goneril's and Regan's deceitfulness counterposed to Lear's trustfulness, and in the final reconciliation of both attitudes through Prospero's magical "revenge."

7. The passage from *The Confidence Man* ironically echoes St. Paul, who warned against the overly private language ("unknown tongues") of apocalyptic interpretation, while favoring the more open speech of prophecy, i.e., the language of edification:

For he that speaketh in an unknown tongue speaketh not unto men, but unto God; for no man understandeth him; howbeit in the spirit he speaketh mysteries.

But he that prophesieth speaketh unto men to edification, and exhortation, and comfort.

He that speaketh in an unknown tongue edifieth himself; but he that prophesieth edifieth the church.

I would that ye all spake with tongues, but rather that ye prophesied: for greater is he that prophesieth than he that speaketh with tongues, except he interpret, that the church may receive edification.

. . . except ye utter by the tongue words easy to be understood how shall it be known what is spoken? for ye shall speak into the air. (1 Cor. 14:2, 3, 4, 5, 9)

In this warning Paul is sometimes represented as attempting to curb a tendency to intellectualize Christian doctrine; the tendency had been developed by Gnostics eager to convert the precepts of Christian faith into an esoteric philosophy and turn its practice into a mystery cult.

V. *Identification*

1. A pictorial example of this sort used to appear on the paper wrapping of the old Uneeda biscuit box. It showed the figure of an aged fisherman holding a smaller biscuit box on which the same old fisherman was reproduced holding a smaller box, and so on.

On a loftier plane, the psychoanalyst Dr. Theodor Reik discovers the inset pattern to be central to an esthetic principle in Goethe's art—which describes the phenomenon of "recurrent reflection"—and pre-empts the observation for his own purposes:

The poet speaks on several occasions of this term, which he borrowed from entoptics. In one essay he tells us that recurrent reflections "not only keep the past alive, but even raise it to a higher existence." He reminds us of the entoptic phenomena "which likewise do not pale as they pass from mirror to mirror, but are actually kindled thereby." In a letter about obscure passages in *Faust* (to Iken, September 23, 1827) he observes: "Since we have many experiences that cannot be plainly expressed or communicated, I have long adopted the method of revealing the secret meaning to attentive readers by images that confront one another and are, so to speak, reflected in one another." I believe that the same procedure that Goethe adopted for literary purposes can, *mutatis mutandis*, with necessary changes, be used on occasion in scientific psychological work, in order to "reveal the secret meaning." *Listening with the Third Ear* (1952), p. 421.

2. Kenneth Burke, *A Grammar of Motives* (1945), pp. 511–512.

VI. The Ideal

1. Sigmund Freud, *Beyond the Pleasure Principle* (trans. J. Strachey, 1950), pp. 47–48.
2. *Ibid*, p. 50.
3. C. S. Lewis, *A Preface to Paradise Lost* (1942), pp. 72–73.
4. F. O. Matthiessen, *American Renaissance* (1941), p. 275.
5. W. P. Ker, *Epic and Romance* (1922), pp. 7–8.
6. Kenneth Burke, *Attitudes Toward History*, I (1937), pp. 44–46.
7. Walter W. Greg, *Pastoral Poetry and Pastoral Drama* (1906), p. 2.
8. William Empson, *English Pastoral Poetry* (1938), pp. 198–199.
9. Ernst Cassirer, *The Myth of the State* (1946), pp. 44–49.

Index

42467   809.93
                         H75

Date Due

DEC 5 '72			
DEC 19 '72			
MAY 1 2 '76			
APR 11 1990			

NYACK MISSIONARY COLLEGE
NYACK, NEW YORK